Election Attitude

HOW INTERNET VOTING LEADS TO A STRONGER DEMOCRACY

John R. Patrick

Attitude
LLC

ISBN: 0692684433
ISBN 13: 9780692684436

Praise for Election Attitude

John Patrick makes a very strong case for serious development of an online voting system for the US. He makes it clear that naysayers are comparing the risks of online voting to perfection rather than the existing unreliable systems. We can do this.

Vint Cerf, Internet Pioneer

At IBM we believe blockchain technology has potential well beyond digital currency. John Patrick's vision in *Election Attitude* highlights a very interesting possibility - using a blockchain to store votes securely.

Jerry Cuomo, IBM Fellow and Vice President, Blockchain Technologies

A report on an Internet voting pilot for the military compared the Internet voting system to a perfect system, not to the current broken system. The latter comparison would have been favorable toward Internet voting. There is nothing we can do to fix the current system. As *Election Attitude* describes, with Internet voting, we can do a lot better.

Dave Farber, formerly Chief Technologist at the U.S. Federal Communications Commission, Trustee of the Electronic Frontier Foundation, and member of the Verified Voting Board of Advisors.

Election Attitude is a call for a model of pioneering courage which built our great nation – the USA. We can shop and bank online, why can't we vote online? John shows the fear mongers and Luddites are wrong when they say Internet voting can't be done. The best minds in computer science have invented top quality security systems for Internet voting. They are being used around the world without hackers tampering with the vote totals. Other countries are already voting securely online. Now it's up to us to demand Internet voting, starting with our state and local leaders.

William J. Kelleher, Ph.D., Political Science Professor and Author of Internet Voting Now: Here's How, Here's Why, So You Can Kiss Citizens United Goodbye

John Patrick convincingly argues for disrupting our most basic of rights, the citizen vote, with Internet voting. He questions, through a historical discussion, policy issues, debates, and future modeling, the fairness and integrity of not taking action to revise and use current technology in the voting process. A must read.

James Neal, Former Vice President for Information Services and University Librarian at Columbia University and President-Elect, American Library Association

Internet voting is inevitable. It will broaden voter participation, help educate the electorate and reduce the influence of Big Money in our political process. As the founder of Shareholder.com, I saw how quickly and effectively public corporations embraced electronic proxy voting by shareholders. John Patrick's book provides a thoughtful framework for how Internet voting can improve the election of our public officials.

Ronald H. Gruner, Founder Alliant Computer and Shareholder.com

The US should establish a national task force to encourage and support Internet Voting pilot projects. This would accelerate the option for voters to cast their ballots online within the next decade. The technical obstacles facing this challenge are minuscule compared with seeking breakthroughs in the fight against cancer. We need to breach the chasm between the ubiquitous use of technology in people's lives and the need to align and integrate the voting experience with the modern world. John Patrick's book dispels the myth that Internet Voting is an unreachable goal.

Conny B. McCormack, former Chief Election Official for Los Angeles County, CA and author of "Democracy Re-booted: The Future of Technology in Elections."

Election Attitude documents many of the most important discussions surrounding Internet technology quite evenly. Still the book is an unapologetic advocacy platform for an election attitude for voting. John shows the Internet has been successful for more than a decade at collecting millions of votes without any frightful disasters. I am convinced John's position of increased access and human hands-free delivery of ballots will improve voting. The security problems are real, but there are many new solutions. John brings together ideas and experiences which can improve the way we develop and deploy voting technology.

Ted Selker, Visiting Scientist at the Center for Information Technology in Interest of Society at UC Berkeley and Past Co-chair of the Caltech/MIT Voting Technology Project

Also by John R. Patrick

Net Attitude: What it is, How to Get it, and Why it is More Important than Ever (2016)

Health Attitude: Unraveling and Solving the Complexities of Healthcare (2015)

Net Attitude: What It Is, How to Get It, and Why Your Company Can't Survive without It (2001)

Dedication

This book is dedicated to my loving wife, Joanne, whose patience allows me time to devote to writing. I am thankful for her perusal, edits, and suggestions.

Preface

I have been a registered American voter for 52 years. Voting evokes memories of stepping into the voting booth, pulling a big red lever to the right to close the privacy curtain, casting my votes by flipping metal levers, pulling the big red lever to the left to record my votes and open the curtain. Voting technology has changed dramatically since the days of mechanical levers. The last few times I voted, it was either with an absentee ballot or a paper ballot inserted into an optical scanner.

One day in early 2016, I was having lunch with Tom Lutz, a college classmate of mine from Lehigh University. I was telling him about my newest book, *Net Attitude*. We also discussed another book I am writing about home automation called *Home Attitude*. He said both books sounded interesting, but what he thought could be even more interesting was a book entitled *Election Attitude*. I immediately liked his idea.

I started preliminary research on the topic and discovered systems for registration and voting in America are antiquated and often prone to error. I began to think of "election attitude" as an idea including a more modern approach to voter registration and the potential to significantly increase both the ease of registration and subsequent participation. Hence, I began writing this book about both the current processes for registration and voting in the United States, and a vision of how voting and registration could be improved.

In the context of the rapidly developing 2016 political scene and the many changes taking place in the voter registration process, I became curious about the part the Internet could play in the voting process. Today, the Internet touches most aspects of our lives, adding a lot of value and helping to simplify our lives.

We go online to shop, bank, take courses, enjoy entertainment, plan travel, make reservations for dinner or a show, and examine our electronic health records. We keep abreast of the news, particularly today's politics, but voting on the Internet is elusive. Voting is an important component of democracy, but it escapes the advantages of current Internet technology.

At the federal, state, and local levels, Americans elect more than a half-million public officials. Some are elected using a mail ballot, but most voting takes place at polling places. Other than in a few isolated trials, none is elected using Internet technology.

By comparison, consider retail sales in the United States. In 2015, total retail sales were approximately $4.7 trillion dollars.[1] Seven and a half percent of the sales were processed through the Internet. Although seven percent may seem low, the growth of Internet sales has been double digits per year since 1995. Retail sales using the Internet have grown from zero to more than $340 billion.[2] E-commerce is more than "click here to buy". All processes associated with e-commerce, including search, order, pay, track, return, and feedback have been greatly enhanced by use of the Internet. The same cannot be said about voting. The United States has one of the lowest voter participation rates in the world.[3] The Internet has the potential to make it easier to register and vote, resulting in expanded participation. Increased involvement could make outcomes more representative of the citizenry.

In many cases, opinion polls show citizen support for a particular issue. Despite the people's support, the issue is then defeated by the citizens' elected representatives. Following are some examples:

For 20 years, the Pew Research Center tracked public opinion on gun rights and gun control. A survey by CNN and Opinion Research Corporation International indicated 86% of the public supported some form of background checks not currently required for gun sales.[4] Even though numerous other polls showed similar results,[5] on April 17, 2013, the U.S. Senate voted against a background check proposal 54 to 46.[6] On June 20, 2016, following the worst mass shooting in the U.S., in Orlando, Florida, the Senate voted down four gun control provisions. Sixty votes were required. Two of the bills received 53 Yeas, one got 44, and one got 47.[7]

Another example is some state legislatures voted to outlaw automobile dealerships from selling the Tesla electric vehicle. This is despite the fact in Consumer Reports Magazine the Tesla Model S is the highest evaluated car and has the highest consumer satisfaction rating of any automobile.[8] The legislators decided the priority was to protect the automobile dealers from new competition.

Another instance of public officials taking action not supported by their electorate is eight cities which have either suspended operations or banned Uber from providing the highly popular car ride service.[9] I believe our elected officials are not listening to those they represent. Internet based polls of randomly selected citizens on specific issues could enable elected officials to hear citizens' voices more clearly and better represent the constituencies who care about specific issues.

Another reality is the closing of polling places throughout the country in order to reduce staff and save money. An additional reason to eliminate them is some historically have low voter turnout. In the 2016 Presidential election, this could be an erroneous gesture. However, in this year's contest and all of those beyond, including those for local officials, Internet voting, were it employed, could vastly improve and facilitate the process. It could eliminate errors and, most important, increase participation in choosing office holders who will truly represent their constituencies. In his Gettysburg Address, President Abraham Lincoln extolled the virtues of America's representative democracy. He said, "...government of the people,... by the people, for the people, shall not perish from the earth."[10] I believe he meant all the people, not just some of the people.

The focus of *Election Attitude* is on the processes and technology enabling registration, voting, and reporting election results. I believe there is a better way to select officials compared to today's methods. There are interesting election and voting issues throughout the world, but the scope of *Election Attitude* is limited to the United States.

Table of Contents

CHAPTER 1
Voting in America

A merica was founded as a constitutional republic. Democracy came later, but a democracy did not originate with the founding of the United States. The word democracy was not mentioned in the Declaration of Independence or the U.S. Constitution. The term democracy was derived from two Greek words: "demos", the people, and "kratia", power or authority.[11] In other words, democracy is a form of government which gives power to the people. Both how the power is given and to whom it is given have changed through the years. Democracy evolved through many debates to a system of government whereby people voted for political leaders. The intention was for elected leaders to make decisions reflecting the will of the electorate. Voting is at the heart of democracy. Our votes are our voices, and collectively our votes are the voice of the country. Whether it is a vote to increase the local school budget or to elect the President of the United States, all voices are important. This chapter will describe for what we vote and how we register to vote.

What We Vote For

With more than 90,000 elected bodies, mostly boards, and more than a half-million elected officials,[12] votes represent direct input to elected officials about the preferences of citizens and how they want to be governed. The selection process for the President receives high national visibility, but voting for other officials and board members is also important. For details on the number and type of officials we elect, see table 1: Elected Bodies and Officials in the United States.

In addition to voting to elect public officials, state and local ballots often include issues, typically called referenda, which are referred to the electorate for a decision. For example, voters may approve or disapprove school or library budgets, authorize projects such as new roads, libraries, school transportation, or outsourcing of public services. Between 1996 and 2014, Californians voted on 196 ballot initiatives. [13]California allows measures to be placed on the ballot through citizen-led initiatives.[14] It is expected 2016 will be a record-setting year for the number of ballot initiatives in California. Their voters will decide a large number of ballot measures in November, including hot-button issues such as marijuana legalization, increasing the minimum wage, changing the justice system for crime victims, and the level of funding for education. [15]

Table 1. Elected bodies and officials in the United States

	Elected Bodies	Elected Officials
Federal Government	1	
Executive Branch		2
U.S. Senate		100
U.S. House of Representatives		435
State Government	50	
State Legislatures		7,382
Statewide Elected Officers		10,036
State Boards		1,331
County	3,031	58,760
Municipal	19,519	136,159
Town or Township	16,360	125,850
Special Districts	38,266	91,799
School Districts	12,880	90,597
Total	90,107	522,451

Sources: Data on state government officials came from the National Conference of State Legislatures[16]. Data on county, municipal, townships, and districts came from United States Census Bureau.[17] Number of elected officials for 2012 was adapted from Census Bureau data of 1992.[18]

Voter Participation

Despite the importance of voting, only slightly more than half of the people over 18 cast a ballot for President in 2012.[19] The United States population in 2012 was 314.1 million. Those over 18 were 53.6% or 241 million. However, not all of the 241 million were eligible to vote. For example, non-citizens and some persons who are institutionalized or incarcerated cannot register to vote.

According to The Sentencing Project, an organization which advocates fair and effective criminal justice, 5.85 million Americans are denied the right to vote because of laws that prohibit voting by people with felony convictions.[20] Felony disenfranchisement is an obstacle to participation in democratic life. There continues to be wide differences of opinion if this should be changed. Fourteen states allow felons to vote after their prison terms are completed even while they remain on parole or probation.[21] Maine and Vermont have no voting restrictions for people with felony convictions. Virginia, Kentucky, Florida, and Iowa have harsh restrictions.[22] For example, some states impose long waiting periods even after a person has served time and completed their parole and probation requirements. The restrictions are magnified when considering racial disparities in the criminal justice system. According to The Sentencing Project, one of every thirteen African Americans is unable to vote because of felony conviction prohibitions.[23] In Virginia, a state with harsh restrictions, it is one out of five.

In recent years, heightened public awareness of felony disenfranchisement has resulted in successful state reform efforts. Since 1997, 23 states have changed felony disenfranchisement provisions and expanded voter eligibility. This resulted in 940,000 citizens in those states regaining their right to vote.[24] In April 2016, Virginia Governor, Terry McAuliffe, used his executive power to overturn a Civil War era provision in the Virginia Constitution which did not allow felons to vote. After this change, more than 200,000 convicted felons in Virginia had their voting rights restored.[25]

In 2012, after subtracting non-citizens and ineligible felons from the 241 million persons over 18, and adding American citizens living overseas, there were 222.5 million Americans eligible to vote. The eligible voters represented 92.3% of those over 18, but only 63.5% of those eligible registered to vote. There were 129.1 million votes cast in the Presidential election in 2012. This represented 84.3% of registered voters, but the votes represented only 58% of those who were eligible to vote. Nearly 70 million citizens did not register to vote.

The Pew Research Center studied 2012 voter participation in the 34 countries of the Organization for Economic Cooperation and Development (OECD). Twenty-eight nations around the world and six in the OECD have laws making voting compulsory. The OECD countries with mandatory voting are Australia, Belgium, Greece, Luxembourg, Mexico, and Turkey. Compulsory voting laws are not always strictly enforced. When they are, the fine is similar to a parking ticket. However, the presence or absence of compulsory voting can have a dramatic impact on voter turnout. Of the five highest turnout OECD countries in recent elections, three had compulsory voting laws.[26] When Chile changed from compulsory to voluntary voting in 2012, voter participation dropped from 87% to 42%.[27]

In the Pew study, votes cast by those of voting age ranged from 40% in Switzerland, which had voluntary voting, to 89% in Belgium, which had compulsory voting.[28] The United States ranked 31st out of the 34 countries with 53.6% of eligible voters participating. See table 2 for the United States Voter Participation in 2012 and see appendix A for Votes Cast in OECD Countries.

Table 2. United States voter participation in 2012

		% Eligible To Vote	% Who Voted
Population	314.1		
Voting Age (>18)	241.0		53.6%
Non-citizens	20.2		
Ineligible felons	3.4		
Eligible overseas	5.1		
Eligible voters	222.5	92.3%	58.0%
Registered voters	153.1	63.5%	84.3%
Votes Cast	129.1	58.0%	

Source: Voting and Registration in the Election of November 2012[29]. Population data in millions.

The American Government website at UShistory.org is owned by the Independence Hall Association, a nonprofit organization in Philadelphia, PA, founded in 1942.[30] The website has a substantial set of reference and educational materials about American government. The page, "American Political Attitudes and Participation", examines reasons for voter non-participation, suggesting there are institutional barriers impacting voter turnout.[31] The following paragraphs describe the origins of voter registration and some of the most commonly cited reasons for low voter participation according to this organization.

Registration Requirements

The United States Constitution was ratified in 1789 and in it were provisions for voting, initially limited mainly to free, white, male landowners aged 21 or older. The Constitution has been amended twenty-seven times. The first ten Amendments are known as the Bill of Rights, ratified in 1791. The most recent 17 Amendments expanded individual civil rights. A number of these Amendments were written specifically to extend voting rights to different groups of citizens. The Amendments providing voting rights cannot be limited or denied for various reasons. For example, the 15th Amendment (1870) established voting rights without regard to race, color, or previous condition of servitude. The 19th Amendment (1920) gave women the right to vote. The 26th Amendment (1971) reduced the voting age to 18.

The right to vote is a cornerstone of our society. Details of how citizens would vote was left to the states. To be eligible to vote in a federal election in the United States, potential voters must meet certain basic requirements.[32] All states require the following conditions:

- ✓ You must be a U.S. citizen.
- ✓ You must meet your state's residency requirements.
- ✓ You generally have to be 18 years old. In some states 17-year-olds can vote in primaries and/or register to vote if they will be 18 before the general election.
- ✓ You must meet the state's voter registration deadlines.
- ✓ You must meet any additional requirements imposed by some states

Registration deadlines vary considerably. Approximately half the states require people to register between 25 and 30 days before the election and approximately half require 7-14 days. Some states make registration simple. North

Dakota does not require registration to vote, making voting in North Dakota "As easy as pie!".[33] Illinois has a complex registration process. Its regular registration is open year round except during the 27 day period prior to an election and during the 2 day period after each election, except in Chicago where it is one day after.[34]

Additional Requirements

Many states have additional requirements in order to be qualified to register to vote. Some states require specific types of identification be produced at the voting site before a person can vote. Alabama is one of the most difficult states to meet the voting requirements. Votes can be cast only in person on Election Day, unless you have an approved excuse to vote absentee. Alabama requires a photo ID. California is among the states which make it easy to vote. No ID is required. You can vote up to four weeks early and you can vote via an absentee ballot with no excuse required.

In total, 19 states require a photo ID, 19 require an ID but no photo, and 12 states require no ID.[35] Wisconsin's requirement for a photo ID went into effect in 2015. Supporters of the law say it prevents fraud. Opponents say as many as 350,000 previously eligible voters could be disenfranchised, placing a burden on the elderly, the poor and people of color. Opponents filed a lawsuit to eliminate the requirement. In April, 2016, the United States Court of Appeals, in a unanimous decision did not strike down the requirement. However, the Court of Appeals ordered a lower federal court to reconsider the case.[36]

Voting Rights

Voting rights are a highly contentious issue in America. At issue is whether some states intentionally restrict the rights of people to vote. In the early days of elections, only white male land owners over 21 could vote. Voting rights have been greatly expanded since then. However, there are active debates in nearly half of the states concerning whether voter participation should be expanded or restricted. The Brennan Center for Justice at New York University School of Law is a nonpartisan law and policy institute seeking to improve systems of democracy and justice. The Institute keeps track of introduced, pending, active, and passed voting bills and maintains its status in a regularly-updated website.[37]

After the 2010 mid-term elections, legislators in dozens of states introduced scores of laws impacting the ease or difficulty of voting. At the end of 2014, the Institute reported at least 340 expansive bills in progress to increase access to voting. The bills were introduced in 42 states plus the District of Columbia. Twelve states plus the District of Columbia passed 19 expansive bills.

At least 83 restrictive bills were introduced in 29 states.[38] Typical restrictive provisions include reducing early voting periods, eliminating same day registration, and reducing access to absentee ballots. Two states passed restrictive bills. Ohio legislation prohibits individuals who lack identification or a Social Security number from voting even with a provisional ballot. Wisconsin legislation reduced early voting periods and hours.

The Voting Rights Act was passed by Congress in 1965 to ensure state and local governments do not pass laws or policies denying American citizens the equal right to vote based on race. This legislation was designed to ensure all citizens, regardless of their race, an equal opportunity to vote and participate in the democratic process. However, on June 25, 2013, the U.S. Supreme Court overturned a key provision of the Voting Rights Act. The Act had required states to obtain federal approval before making any changes to their election laws.[39] The Federal Government had previously applied the pre-approval process to nine states including Alabama, Alaska, Arizona, Georgia, Louisiana, Mississippi, South Carolina, Texas and Virginia.[40] The provision also applied to scores of counties and municipalities in other states. Since the 2013 Supreme Court ruling, all of these jurisdictions can implement barriers to voting. In Texas, for example, a federal judge found 600,000 registered voters lacked a required photo ID. The judge ruled the requirement making it harder for minorities to vote, was enacted to intentionally discriminate against minorities, and unconstitutionally burdens the right to vote.[41] In late April, 2016, the United States Supreme Court refused to block the photo ID law, but it left open the possibility of doing so in July 2016 if a lower court challenge remains unresolved.[42]

Civil rights groups who say the Voting Rights Act discriminates against black and Hispanic voters had argued it should be blocked because it was struck down by a federal court in 2014 and a three-judge appeals court panel last year. The full U.S. Court of Appeals for the 5th Circuit will hear the case in summer 2016.

The justices said they would reconsider their decision on or after July 20, 2016 if the Appeals Court had not decided the case by then. The outcome of the decision would give state election officials more than three months to prepare voters for the November elections.

On January 16, 2014, Reps. John Conyers (D-Mich.) and James Sensenbrenner (R-Wis.), with Sen. Patrick Leahy (D-Vt.) and others, introduced a bill to strengthen the Voting Rights Act.[43] The Bill contained numerous provisions to strengthen the Voting Rights Act including a requirement jurisdictions which had a record of repeated Voting Rights Act violations must get a federal pre-approval for any election law changes.[44] The Bill died in Congress.[45] Debate on voting requirements continues at the national and state level, but based on the number of bills introduced, I believe the trend is toward expanded voter participation.

Difficulty of Registration.

Many other democracies, such as France and Sweden, make it very easy for a citizen to vote by automatically registering their citizens and alerting them to vote. In contrast, United States citizens must register themselves. The roots of United States voter registration began in the early 19th century.[46] State governments were concerned with the growing participation of foreign-born people voting in local elections.[47] Voter registration was implemented to prevent non-citizens from voting. Another goal was to avoid conflicts, even riots, between election officials and disenfranchised voters. Voter registration accomplished the goals but, at the same time, disenfranchised many poor citizens.[48]

The specter of fraud caused changes which made it more difficult to register. I will discuss voter fraud in chapter 2. Whatever the actual degree of voter fraud, both major parties responded to this concern by making it more difficult for a person to vote. As a result, for more than 100 years, in most states, voter registration has been a prerequisite for voting. However, reforms can have unintended consequences. "American Political Attitudes and Participation", an online course in politics by USHistory.org, cited voter registration difficulty as a factor in reduced voter participation.[49] In 2013, Barry C. Burden and Jacob R. Neiheisel, of the Department of Political Science at the University of Wisconsin-Madison scrutinized this assumption along two dimensions.[50]

First, the researchers determined the effects attributed to registration have not been due to registration per se. They found other factors such as closing dates, residency requirements, roll purging processes, and felon disenfranchisement laws had more effect on voter participation than the requirement for registration itself. Using a variety of modeling techniques, the researchers calculated the pure effect of having to register is approximately 2 percentage points, but this could easily represent an election's failure or success. They concluded the large difference in voter participation rates in the United States compared to other countries cannot be explained by the requirement for registration.

The second dimension Burden and Neiheisel studied was administrative capacity at the local level. In voting districts with adequate staffing of well-trained clerks, registration had no impact on participation. Districts with scarce resources were less able to implement registration requirements and assure registrants they could vote. The well trained clerks could answer voters' questions, assist voters with their registration information, and direct them to the voting line. Some clerks may turn the voter away because they have not been well trained.

In another study, political researchers Rene Rocha and Tetsuya Matsubayashi used state-level data and the Current Population Survey for 1980 to 2010 to analyze the effects of various voter registration laws. They found little evidence to support the belief minority turnout is directly related to voter ID regulations.[51]

In 2012, 6 million Americans did not vote because they missed a registration deadline or didn't know how to register.[52] Supported by a proclamation from the White House, and in partnership with more than 2,100 businesses, organizations, election officials, schools, and civic groups, the National Voter Registration Day organization wants to make sure no one is left out in the future.[53] On September 27, 2016, they will participate in National Voter Registration Day. The goal of on the ground teams, technology, and media efforts will be to create wide spread awareness of voter registration opportunities. The 2015 National Voter Registration Day added 129,851 new registrants nationwide.[54] More than half registered online.

Another voter registration initiative is the Electronic Registration Information Center (ERIC). ERIC is a non-profit corporation governed by a board of directors made up of 16 state members. ERIC streamlines processes to maintain accurate and complete voter rolls. Thirty states plus the District of Columbia now offer online registration. ERIC has helped states identify more than three million out-of-date voter records and more than 140,000 records of individuals who have died since they last voted.[55] ERIC has enabled 700,000 new voters to register online. The member states have been able to improve the accuracy of voter registration data and gain additional benefits. They saw a steep reduction in returned mail, fewer provisional ballots, and significantly reduced registration costs.

Despite cases of restrictive registration in some states, I believe progress is being made. An open question is whether easier and more convenient methods of registration and voting could lead to higher participation. An election attitude suggests the entire process should be as easy as one-click purchasing online.

Difficulty of Absentee Voting

Absentee voting challenges have been shown to affect voter participation. This is particularly true for military personnel and American citizens living outside of the United States. Even if a person is a registered voter, the usual process of voting requires the voter to cast their ballot at the voting precinct. If you are out of town on Election Day, you have to submit an absentee ballot ahead of time. Some states have stringent rules for absentee voting. Nineteen states require an approved excuse. Typical excuses include military deployment, prescheduled travel, or illness which prohibits a voter from leaving the house.[56] In some states, you can vote ahead of time, but have to apply for an absentee ballot in person.[57] Another set of problems arise when the ballots are received at voting precincts. Nearly two percent of the absentee ballots are rejected for various reasons.[58] I will discuss this more in chapter 3.

Frequency of Elections

America has more elected public officials than any other democracy.[59] In the United States, as shown in table 1, we vote for the President and vice-president, senators and representatives, governors, judges, state commissioners, mayors, city council members, and numerous other local officials. Elections are frequent. Someone is being elected to some office almost every week in the United States.[60] Ted Selker, Visiting Scientist at the Center for Information Technology in Interest of Society at UC Berkeley and Past Co-chair of the Caltech/MIT Voting Project, said, "There is hardly a day when there isn't an election in the United States."[61]

In 2016, we will have at least two major elections. In some cases, there will be runoff elections. The need for frequent voting may reduce voter participation. Arend Lijphart is a political scientist specializing in comparative politics, elections and voting systems, democratic institutions, ethnicity, and politics. He is Research Professor Emeritus of Political Science at the University of California, San Diego. Dr. Lijphart said, "The frequency of elections has a strongly negative influence on turnout".[62] I think if voting was more convenient, this might not be true. Dr. Selker added that if voting was easy and became more frequent, people may accept it.

Weekday Voting

In the United States, the national general elections are held on the Tuesday after the first Monday in November in even-numbered years. Although some employers and most state and local offices give employees one or two hours paid time off to vote, it may not be convenient for some who have long commutes. After the 2014 midterm elections, 69% of non-voters said they did not vote because they were stuck at school or work, or were too busy, out of town, sick, or forgot.[63]

Ambassador Andrew Young, Senator Bill Bradley and Congressman Jack Kemp formed a public policy group called Why Tuesday? Why Tuesday? has prompted the passage of the Saturday Voting Act in San Francisco and a study by the U.S. GAO about the feasibility of implementing Weekend Voting in the United States.[64] Many countries, including Australia (81.0 percent turnout), Greece (69.4 percent turnout), and Brazil (80.6 percent turnout) have weekend election days.[65] E-commerce occurs 24/7. An election attitude would include easy online registration and convenient voting via websites or mobile, on any day of the week with extended hours for voting. An election attitude could potentially increase voter participation and representation of the electorate.

The Motor-Voter Law

In 1993, Congress passed the National Voter Registration Act, more commonly known as the "Motor-Voter" Law.[66] Under the Act, states are required to facilitate voter registration when applying for a driver's license. This legislation took effect in 1995, but the impact is mixed. Florida reported the most transactions of any state between October 1994 and May 1996. The Florida voter rolls added 2.15 million new voters.[67] However, due to deaths and people moving out of the state, the net addition to the rolls was only one million. California reported 884,000 transactions with a net decrease in registration of 200,000 voters.[68] Despite California's voting-age population increase of 400,000 during the same period, the proportion of voters registered actually declined from 77.7 percent in October 1994 to 75.1 percent in March 1996.[69]

Supporters had estimated an additional 50 million people would register as a result of the Motor-Voter Law[70] since it requires states to facilitate voter registration. Facilitating meant when a person received a driver license or made a change to an existing one, he or she was asked if they would like to register to vote.

A reform to modernize voter registration which has the potential to dramatically increase registration rates is automatic voter registration (AVR). AVR legislation has passed in California, Oregon, Vermont, and West Virginia, and dozens more are considering the idea.[71] As of April 2016, 28 states plus the District of Columbia have considered AVR. The potential to go well beyond Motor-Voter is significant. When a citizen has an interaction with any government agency, his or her voter information can be electronically, accurately, and securely transmitted to election officials.

Problems at the Polling Places

Another factor affecting voter participation is the conditions at the polling places. Availability of ballots and working voting machines in sufficient numbers for high voter participation are prerequisites which sometimes do not exist. I will discuss those issues in more detail in chapter 2.

Conclusion

America has low voter participation. Only 58% of the eligible citizens cast their votes in the last Presidential election. To be a strong representative democracy, the United States must have elections which include a representation of the population. The result would be a stronger voice for the people and a stronger democracy. Despite initiatives to improve American voter turnout, participation has continued to decline. The mid-term election of 2014 had the lowest turnout in 72 years.[72] The lively debates of 2016 have led to record participation levels in the primaries, beating records as far back to 1980.[73] It remains to be seen if the general election will show a similar increase. I believe increased use of technology in the voting process could bring about the most effective change. These tools, which have empowered consumers in their daily lives, could enable easier registration, more convenient voting, and a host of new ways of participating in American democracy. The next chapter focuses on how we vote today.

CHAPTER 2

How We Vote Today

I n chapter 1, I discussed the numerous issues in the voter registration process. Many issues also exist with the voting methods. Over decades, even though there have been significant changes in how we vote, some of the methods used varied widely and affected voter participation.

In 1992, for example, there were five different voting systems in operation in the United States. The percentage of use of each type of system is: 39% punch card voting machines, 29% mechanical lever machines, 15% paper ballots with optical scanning, 5% electronic voting machines, and 4% hand-counted paper ballots.[74] In 2000, use of the punch card voting system was still high at 31%.[75] Use of mechanical lever machines declined to 17% as technology began to have an impact on the voting process. Election sites using paper ballots with optical scanning doubled to 29.5%. The installation and use of electronic voting machines nearly tripled to 12.5%. The use of hand-counted paper ballots decreases to only 1.5%. See figure 1 for details on voting systems used between 1992 and 2012

During the late 1990s, the millennium changing year 2000, referred to as Y2K, was the subject of great concern among all users of information technology systems. Most computer applications and databases treated dates as six-digit fields of information. Two digits were allocated for the day, two for the month, and two for the year. The year should have been represented by four digits, but many software developers were not thinking that far ahead during the early development of computer software. In the start up days of computers, storage space was extremely expensive and therefore limited in size. It was clear to software developers and early adopters the number 99 in the year field meant 1999. However, as the year 2000 approached, the question arose whether or not computer software would know whether 00 meant 1900 or 2000. Many scenarios of computer programs were unpredictable. For example, if a computer program calculated how many years there were between 1995 and 1985, the math was easy. Subtracting 85 from 95 yielded ten years. However, if the question was how many years are there between 1985 and 2000, a program would subtract 85 from 00. The result would have been -85. What the software would do next could not be predicted. Experts warned the integrity of financial data and other types of transactional data could be at risk. Large organizations around the world spent billions of dollars to modify or replace their software and prepare for the year 2000. Fortunately, by the end of 1999, most organizations were prepared, and relatively few problems occurred which could not be repaired easily.[76] As it turned out, the Y2K's biggest unpredictable happening occurred during the 2000 Presidential election.

Election Year 2000

What happened in the 2000 Presidential election between George W. Bush and Vice President Al Gore was unprecedented. This election clearly demonstrated the American system of elections, the hallmark of our democracy, had some serious flaws. In Palm Beach County, Florida, voters were presented with a "butterfly ballot", a punch card ballot with names down both sides and a single column of rectangular punch holes in the center. By punching out a rectangle, the tabulating equipment should detect the hole and count the vote. In some cases, the small, paper rectangle, called a chad, may not have been completely punched out, and the vote was not counted. The other problem with the butterfly ballots was the candidate names were not aligned with the places to indicate the vote. Many voters were confused and unknowingly selected a different candidate than they intended. The ballots were so confusing to many voters 19,235 people, or four percent, voted for more than one Presidential candidate. As a result, their votes were not counted.[77]Chad went from an unfamiliar country most people had never heard of to a famous word. The many variations of the degree to which a chad might be in question led Palm Beach County, Florida officials to refer to a glossary of terms about chads. They referred to it as chadology. The variations included hanging, dimpled, pregnant, swinging-door, and tri chads.[78]

After a month of recounts and review of ballots, Vice President Gore supporters asked the Florida Supreme Court to recount votes again. This time, the recount would be only in certain counties where they thought Gore would gain votes, and to not include counties where they thought Bush would gain.[79] The United States Supreme Court, in *Bush v. Gore*, ruled the strategy illegal. Following the Court's 5-4 decision, George W. Bush was declared the winner over Vice President Al Gore by 537 votes. Gore won the popular vote by more than a half-million votes but, because of the vote count supported by the Supreme Court, lost the electoral college vote by five votes.

The problems with the 2000 election were much larger than Florida's "hanging chads". In the *Scientific American* article, "Fixing the Vote: Electronic Voting Machines Promise to Make Fixing Elections More Accurate Than Ever before, but Only If Certain Problems—with the Machines and the Wider Electoral Process—Are Rectified", Ted Selker, Visiting Scientist at the Center for Information Technology in Interest of Society at UC Berkeley and past co-chair of the Caltech/MIT voting technology project, said, "The total of ballots not counted in the 2000 election nationwide ranged from four to six million, more than two percent of the 150 million registered voters."[80] Selker explained, "There were three reasons accounting for the huge number of lost votes. The largest problem was errors in the registration database preventing one and a half to three million people from voting. More than 70,000 registered voter names were purged".[81] Another one and a half to two million votes were lost due to equipment problems or poor ballot design. The final reason for lost ballots, according to the United States Census Bureau, was polling place problems.[82] Long lines, creating many hours of wait time, in some cases five to six hours, caused some voters to give up and leave without voting. The bottom line is we will never know what the outcome of the 2000 election would have been if these problems had not existed and all the potential votes were counted without error. We just don't know. The voting system let us down.

Equipment Upgrades

Following the 2000 election debacle, the United States Congress passed the Help America Vote Act of 2002.[83] Among the provisions of this Act was the allocation of $3.9 billion to help jurisdictions upgrade from voting systems using lever machines and punch cards to systems with electronic displays or optical scanners.[84] These modern methods are commonly referred to as electronic voting (e-voting) systems.

Mechanical lever machines were completely phased out by 2010. By 2012, paper ballots with optical scanning had grown to 56% of use and electronic voting machines to 39%. Hand-counted paper ballots remained at 4% and punch card systems had virtually disappeared.[85] The e-voting machines were not connected to the Internet for remote voting. Voting from home or away from the voting precinct continued to be primarily facilitated by paper ballots and the United States Postal System.

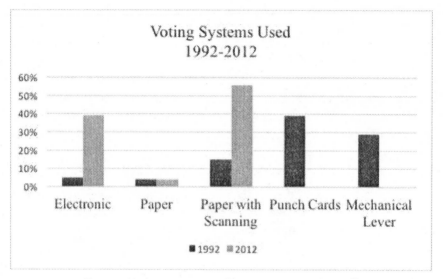

Figure 1. Voting systems used between 1992 and 2012[86]

A survey of the states after the 2014 elections showed variations in the type of voting technologies used. Eighteen states reported deploying 189,441 Direct Recording Electronic machines.[87] The machines are an electronic implementation of the old mechanical lever systems. They do not use a ballot. The possible choices are displayed to the voter on the front of the machine and the voter directly makes choices with the touch of a finger. A keyboard is often provided to allow for write-in votes. The voter's choices are stored in the machines on a memory cartridge, diskette, or smart-card. A criticism of the Direct Recording Electronic machines is they do not provide voter verifiable paper receipts. Another 21 States reported using 69,901 of the new machines with voter-verified paper audit trails. The most widely deployed technology was the mark sense system. Voters mark their choice on a paper ballot by filling a rectangle, circle or oval, or by completing an arrow. The voter then inserts the ballot into a scanner which determines which marks are counted as votes or optical scanners which read voter marked paper ballots. Forty-four states reported using 265,267 of this type of voting machine.[88]

Although there will not be any more hanging chads determining the outcome of future elections, the technology upgrades made possible by the Help America Vote Act are not a panacea in my opinion. The Federal Government provided the funding to replace the punch cards and mechanical lever machines but it did not provide funding to maintain the equipment as it aged. Many of the electronic machines are now nearly 15 years old.

The American Voting Experience

In January 2014, "The American Voting Experience: Report and Recommendations of the Presidential Commission on Election Administration" was released.[89] The Report was the result of six months of public hearings and consultations with state and local election officials, academic experts, and organizations involved in voting or election administration. The goal of the Report and its recommendations was to significantly improve the American voter's experience and promote confidence in the administration of U.S. elections. The report opened with a description of America's voting system.

> The United States runs its elections unlike any other country in the world. Responsibility for elections is entrusted to local officials in approximately 8,000 different jurisdictions. In turn, they are subject to general oversight by officials most often chosen through a partisan appointment or election process. The point of contact for voters in the polling place is usually a temporary employee who has volunteered for one-day duty and has received only a few hours of training. These defining features of our electoral system, combined with the fact that Americans vote more frequently on more issues and offices than citizens anywhere else, present unique challenges for the effective administration of elections that voters throughout the country expect and deserve.[90]

The Presidential Commission made four recommendations.

1) Modernization of the registration process through continued expansion of online voter registration and expanded state collaboration in improving the accuracy of voter lists

2) Measures to improve access to the polls through expansion of the period for voting before the traditional Election Day, and through the selection of suitable, well-equipped polling place facilities, such as schools

3) State-of-the-art techniques to assure efficient management of polling places, including tools the Commission is publicizing and recommending for the efficient allocation of polling place resources

4) Reforms of the standard-setting and certification process for new voting technology to address soon-to-be antiquated voting machines and to encourage innovation and the adoption of widely available off-the-shelf technologies[91]

The missing ingredient from the Presidential Commission Report was the funding needed to implement the recommendations. In 2015, The Brennan Center for Justice published a detailed report on what the Presidential Commission on Election Administration described as an "impending crisis ... from the widespread wearing out of voting machines purchased a decade ago".[92] This Report referred to the need for "new voting technology to address soon-to-be antiquated voting machines". [93]To prepare the extensive report, the Brennan Center surveyed more than 100 specialists familiar with voting technology, including voting machine vendors, independent technology experts, and election officials in all 50 states.

The Center reviewed scores of news reports, press releases, legislation, meeting minutes, and other publicly available materials to develop an accurate view of the extent of the crisis. I have edited the summary of the finding as follows:

Unlike voting machines used in past eras, today's systems were not designed to last for decades. In part this is due to the pace of technological change. No one expects a laptop to last for 10 years. Although the computers used with today's voting machines debuted at the beginning of this century, many were designed and engineered in the 1990s.

It is impossible to say how long any particular machine will last. Experts agree for those purchased since 2000, the expected lifespan for the core components of electronic voting machines is between 10 and 20 years. For most systems it is probably closer to 10 than 20.

The majority of machines in use today are either close to or exceed these estimates. Forty-three states are using voting machines which are at least 10 years old. In 14 states, machines are 15 or more years old. Nearly every state is using some machines which are no longer manufactured and election officials struggle to find replacement parts.

The longer jurisdictions delay purchasing new equipment, the higher the risk becomes. The biggest risk is increased failures and crashes, which can lead to long lines and lost votes.

Older machines can have serious security and reliability flaws which are unacceptable today. For example, Virginia recently decertified a voting system used in 24 percent of precincts after finding an external party could access the machine's wireless features to record voting data or inject malicious data.

Some problems can shake public confidence. Several election officials mentioned "flipped votes" on touch screen machines, where a voter touches the name of one candidate, but the machine registers it as a selection for another.

Election officials who believe they need to buy new machines do not have sufficient resources. Election jurisdictions in at least 31 states want to purchase new voting machines in the next five years. Officials from 22 of these states said they did not know where they would get the money to pay for them.

Based upon recent contracts and assessments provided by election officials, the Brennan Center estimates the initial national cost of replacing equipment over the next few years could exceed $1 billion, though that could be partially offset by lower operating costs and better contracts than are currently used in many jurisdictions.

As election jurisdictions diverge in how they respond to the crisis, the Report identified an increasing divide among, and even within, states.

The diverse response to the crisis may jeopardize ensuring elections can be conducted without system failures and disruption.

A preliminary analysis by the Brennan Center lends support to an equity concern expressed by some officials. Without federal or state funding, wealthier counties will replace aging machines, while poorer counties will be forced to use them far longer than they should.[94]

On April 29, 2016, United States Congressman Hank Johnson of Georgia introduced the "Verifying Optimal Tools for Elections Act of 2016". This Act would allocate more than $125 million dollars in Help America Vote Act grants to assist states in replacing old, outdated voting machines. An important provision of the bill specifies non-proprietary, open source software as an imperative for the next generation voting machines to ensure new technology can be easily managed, reviewed, and improved.[95] The legislation would allocate funds for educational resources for election officials and encourage states to make grant requests for systems using open source software. As of May 2016, the Bill has been referred to the House Committee on House Administration and the House Committee on Science & Space.

In addition to the crisis with aging technology, there are other contributing factors in the current voting system. Lack of the necessary number of ballots to meet high voter turnout and the inadequate number of voting machines at polling places also contribute to the crisis. The following paragraphs outline other key problems.

Problems at the Polling Places

In some cases, availability of convenient polling places is a problem. Election officials in Arizona in 2016 reduced the number of polling sites as part of a purported budgetary necessity. The 70% reduction in polling places from 200 in 2012 to 60 in 2016 resulted in one polling place per 21,000 voters.[96] Hundreds of thousands of voters appearing for the March 22 primaries were confused, inconvenienced, and outraged at the excessive wait times. Many Arizonans left the polls in disgust.[97] Others waited as much as five hours.[98] Arizona was not alone in reducing the number of polling places. Rhode Island opened only 144 of the state's 419 polling places for the April 2016 primary.[99] Open government advocate John Marion of Common

Cause Rhode Island said, "Voters could be confused because their polling place may have changed from what it was the last time they voted."[100]

In Brooklyn, New York, there was a range of complaints during the April, 2016 primary. Faulty ballot scanners caused continuing interruptions and delays. Inadequate staffing at polling sites and poll workers failing to open up sites on time prevented some people from voting because the voters could not wait. Many voters reported their names were mysteriously missing from the voter rolls, so they were not allowed to vote. The New York City Board of Elections confirmed more than 125,000 Democratic voters in Brooklyn were removed from the rolls.[101] Voters complained there were numerous errors caused by the purging of entire buildings and blocks of voters.[102] The Brooklyn Board of Elections Executive Committee voted to suspend their Chief Clerk without pay pending an internal investigation.[103]

Harris Miller, formerly President of the Information Technology Association of America, a leading industry trade group for information technology companies during the late 1990s, has a lot of experience with the American voting system because the voting machine companies were members of the Association. He is in favor of Internet voting. "Visiting polling places to vote has served us well for many years, but it is time for a more modern approach",[104] he said. Miller pointed out that in addition to aging voting machines, we have aging and ill prepared election workers. Historically, the majority of polling place workers have been women, but as more women began to work outside of the home, the supply of election workers has become strained. I confirmed this with Regina Ofiero, an election worker since 1985. Ms. Ofiero is a moderator at the Danbury High School polling place in Fairfield County, Connecticut. As moderator, she is in effect the manager of the entire voting process at the polling place, including recruiting poll workers. She said that at least 70% of the poll workers are women. Not only are the existing workers aging, but very few young people are expressing interest in the job.

Problems with Ballots

During the March 15, 2016 primaries in Florida, the hanging chad problem was resolved, but other problems with ballots persist and new ones arose. According to the Supervisor of Elections Office, the voters in one precinct in Flagler County were given the wrong ballots, resulting in about 30 people who voted for the wrong county commissioner candidates. Election officials went through every ballot individually and corrected the errors. The county election was not impact-ed and there was no effect on the Presidential race.[105]

In Orange County, Florida, during the 2016 primary, about a dozen of the 251 precincts ran out of ballots. As early as 9 a.m., the Pinecastle Masonic Lodge and several additional precincts ran out of both Democrat and Republican ballots. At some precincts, the order to print more ballots was incorrect. Instead of print-ing more Presidential ballots, more city ballots were printed. Voters were told to come back later. More than a dozen citizens protested outside the Orange County Supervisor of Elections Office. The Supervisor had absentee ballots printed and hand-delivered to voters' homes or at workplaces later in the day. Also, several polling places in Orange County had problems verifying voter registration. The tablet computers used to swipe a voter's driver license had problems connect-ing to the Internet. These locations had to request delivery of printed registration books from the archives.[106]

In Polk County, Florida, a precinct poll worker couldn't find the Democratic primary ballots. When the worker opened the polling place, the volunteer only handed out the Republican ballots and told Democrats they couldn't get a ballot. Voters called the Supervisor of Elections Office, which told the poll worker where to find the ballots. These are a few examples of ballot problems which happened in many states during the 2016 Presidential primary.

Ballot Complexity

All of the current voting methods can be subject to error because they depend on a certain level of a person's knowledge of the voting process. Some ballots are not well designed and can be confusing. Some ballots require a simple choice: vote for A or vote for B. The design of some other ballots is not so straightforward.

In *Voting Technology: The Not-So-Simple Act of Casting a Ballot* (2009), Paul Herrnson, Richard Niemi, and Michael Hanmer reported on their research into the complexities of voting. The authors described election ballots as having curiosities and inconsistencies in their format.

> Ballot instructions, candidate and party listings, party symbols, and, in general, variations that result from a complex and highly decentralized election system provide ample opportunity for all but the most sophisti-cated voters to misunderstand, mismark, or spoil their ballots and for all

voters to feel confused and frustrated. We call attention to the enormous disparity in ballot designs across the states and to individual state designs that are inconsistent and needlessly complex.[107]

The most famous example of ballot complexity is the butterfly ballot problem in Florida in 2000 described earlier. However, there are many other examples. Herrnson, Niemi, and Hanmer, an interdisciplinary group of experts on American elections, political behavior, human-computer interaction, and psychology, assessed numerous voting systems in 2008. They evaluated five commercially available voting systems in terms of ease of use, speed, and accuracy. They explored the interaction between the format of ballots and voter behavior and found some features contributed to greater clarity, but others led to confusion and error. Hopefully, their research will inform manufacturers of voting systems, ballot designers, political observers, and election officials, and help them build voting systems which accurately record and count the choices we make.

Machine Failures

As described in the Report from the 2014 Presidential Commission, many voting machines are old and in danger of failing. The majority of the voting machines are either electronic touchscreen, mark sense scanners, or optical scanners. The voting machines contain a computer which uses Microsoft Windows. Most use Windows XP which has had no new security updates or patches since 2014. If a security exposure is detected, Microsoft no longer provides support. Some states have voting machines running on Windows 2000 which has not been supported since 2010.

The computer hardware in most voting machines contains technology nearly as old as 18 year old voters. Some of the systems use PCMCIA storage cards. The credit card sized cards cost about $100 and store approximately a half million bytes of data. In contrast, a USB thumb drive today costs less than $10 and stores 32 billion bytes of data. *Wired* reported in an article, "The Dismal State of America's Decade-Old Voting Machines", one county in Florida relies on a slow, outdated, and hard-to-find analog modem which transmits voting results at a snail's pace of a few thousand bytes of information per second.[108] This may explain why some precincts are very late in reporting data the TV stations depend on for their election coverage.

The *Wired* story reported numerous issues with the old voting machines. For example, "One of the most serious problems with aging machines is they are prone to crashes and screen freezes, which can lead to long lines at polling stations and disenfranchised voters who leave without casting ballots."[109]

The most serious issues with old machines are lack of reliability and integrity. Malfunctioning machines can record votes improperly or even fail to record votes. For example, electronic touchscreen voting machines can lose calibration. When this happens, a person may see a candidate's name on the screen, but when voters touch the screen, they may have selected a candidate above or below the one for which they wanted to vote. The *Wired* story said, "Numerous voting districts have reported calibration problems over the years with seemingly 'flipping' votes—that is, recording a vote for a different candidate than the one the voter selected onscreen."[110]

With some voting systems, the machine may operate as designed, but the design may be flawed. For example, mark-sense scanners are designed to look for oval or elliptical targets on the paper ballot. If the voter used a pencil to fill in the target, the corresponding choice is counted. However, some voters do not understand the instructions, and rather than filling in the target, they put a circle around it, underline it, or put an X through it thereby causing the scanner to not record the vote.[111] The more modern optical character recognition scanners actually look at the ballot and can determine what the voter intended.

Security

Despite the upgrades from punch card machines to electronic display and scanning technologies found in e-voting, concerns about the integrity of these systems persist. Some anti-Internet voting activists have raised concerns which dwarf the hanging chad issue of 2000. In *Broken Ballots*, Douglas W. Jones, Computer Science Professor, University of Iowa, and Barbara Simons, a retired IBM researcher, described how both legislation and the regulatory structure governing voting systems have been ineffective addressing technological risks such as security, privacy, and verifiability.[112] They say, "These risks are often not understood by election administrators and regulators."[113] The authors highlight a series of technology and process failures resulting in reasons to question whether the official vote count always represents the intent of the voters. Some computer scientists are skeptical about Internet voting, but *Broken Ballots* casts significant doubt whether e-voting machines can be trusted either.

Alternative Methods of Voting

Even though the vast majority of votes in America are cast in person on Election Day, most states provide a method for eligible voters to cast a ballot prior to Election Day. These early votes may occur during a defined early voting period or by requesting an absentee ballot. However, in 13 states, early voting is not available and an excuse is required to request an absentee ballot. The Center for Democracy and Election Management at American University reported 37 states allow some form of voting by mail.[114] Often called convenience balloting, there are three types of voting alternatives to appearing at a polling place on election day.[115]

1) Early voting is allowed in 37 states and the District of Columbia. Any qualified voter may cast a ballot in person during a designated period prior to Election Day. No excuse or justification is required.

2) Absentee voting is available in most states. All states will mail an absentee ballot to voters who are eligible under state rules and request one. The voter may return the ballot by mail or in person. In 19 states, an excuse is required to obtain an absentee ballot, while 27 states and the District of Columbia permit any qualified voter to vote absentee without offering an excuse. Some states maintain a permanent absentee ballot list. Once a voter asks to be added to the list, she or he will automatically receive an absentee ballot for all future elections.

3) Voting by mail has resulted in increased voter participation in the states which allow it.[116] The voting jurisdictions using mail ballots enjoy significant savings associated with the cost of operating polling places and for the storage and maintenance of voting machines. Oregon has adopted a mail-in balloting system. Since 2000, Oregon has sent ballots to every registered voter about two weeks before Election Day. Oregon is a national leader in voter turnout with 97% of voters using the mail-in system.[117] After Washington made the change to all mail-in balloting, their turnout improved to 13th best in 2012, from 15th in 2008.[118] When Colorado adopted mail voting, their turnout increased to roughly 2 million people in 2014, up from 1.8 million in 2010.[119]

Other states, including Florida, Kansas, Minnesota, Missouri, Montana, Nevada, New Mexico, and North Dakota allow mail-in voting.[120] Absentee voting by mail was unique for years, but then some states, such as Oregon and

Washington, began to offer voting by mail for anyone with no excuse required. They call it Vote by Mail. Some confusion remains about the difference between absentee voting and voting by mail. There really is no difference. It is all Vote by Mail. In Florida, they are in the process of renaming their absentee voting program to Vote by Mail. Some states allow the mail-in voting only for ballot questions, not for electing government officials.[121] Some states are hesitant to make such a switch to Vote By Mail. Reasons range from desire to maintain status quo to concerns about the possibility of higher rates of voter fraud or coercion.

Regardless of the reason a voter may have to vote by mail, privacy must be maintained. A very straightforward process makes it possible. Voters make their choices on a paper ballot and insert the ballot in a sealed ballot envelope. The voter places the ballot envelope in another envelope, puts his or her name on the outside of the envelope and mails it to the voting precinct. Upon receipt of the envelope, the voting precinct marks the voter as having voted and the ballot envelope is given to the people who count the votes. There is no linkage between the voter's identity and the voter's ballot. The two envelopes go their separate ways and the voter's privacy is protected. The only drawback is if an error was made on the ballot, it may not be possible to be corrected. There are other ways the process can produce errors. First is the reliance on the United States Postal Service and local voting precinct administrative capabilities. Human error can prevent the ballot from getting from mail to the right place to be counted. Ballots can get lost in the mail or physically damaged along the way.

Voting Survey

The Election Assistance Commission is an independent bipartisan agency of the United States government created by the Help America Vote Act of 2002. The Commission serves as a national clearinghouse and resource for information regarding election administration. In 2014, they issued a Report entitled, "Election Administration and Voting Survey Comprehensive Report", which was delivered to Congress in June 2015.[122] The Report is based on two questionnaires sent to all States: (1) A quantitative instrument, the Election Administration and Voting Survey, and (2) A qualitative Statutory Overview, which asks States to report on their election laws, definitions, and procedures.

The survey discovered voting on Election Day remains the most popular form of voting with 60.6% of voters casting a regular ballot in person. Others voted by domestic absentee ballot (17.5%); by early voting before Election Day (10.7%); and by mail voting (7.6%). In addition, provisional ballots were cast when there were questions about a given voter's eligibility, such as when a voter refuses to show a photo ID (0.9%). A small remainder voted by absentee ballot as overseas or uniformed services voters (0.2%). The states who reported the data were unable to classify approximately 2.5% of the ballots.[123]

Some further clarification of the terms used in the Survey help further explain their meaning. Domestic absentee ballots are mailed to U.S. residents who are not able to be at their polling location on Election Day. Some states require an approved excuse for casting such a ballot. Some others do not. Early voting means in-person voting for a period of time, typically two weeks, before Election Day. Mail voting means votes placed by mail because of voter preference, not because they were unable to go to the polling location. The terminology can be confusing. Voting by mail, mail voting, vote by mail, and absentee voting are all essentially the same thing. In 2014, the states sent more than 29 million domestic absentee ballots to voters. Sixty-six percent of the ballots were returned by the voters and counted. Almost ten million were not returned. Absentee ballots, while simple and cost saving, are also believed to be the most common source of vote fraud in this country.[124]

Provisional ballots are a small percentage of the total, but in 2014 accounted for almost 900,000 ballots. Thousands of voters appeared at a polling place but the poll workers raised an issue. It could be the voter did not have or forgot to bring a voter ID. Some may have a discrepancy in their voter registration data, such as an address change or error. In some cases, a voter may have gone to the wrong polling place. In all of these cases, a voter could fill out a provisional ballot. States counted 80.3% of their provisional ballots. Approximately 171,000 provisional votes were rejected. The most common reason for the rejections was the voter was not properly registered.

Voting by Military Personnel and Civilians Overseas

Voting by military personnel and civilians overseas has been a problem for many years. These voting problems are low voter participation and a high level of rejection of mailed ballots. The U.S. Constitution put the states in charge of administering elections, not only for their own state and local elections, but for federal elections as well. The subject of administering voter participation for those overseas was not addressed. Congress finally faced the problem and passed the

Uniformed and Overseas Citizens Absentee Voting Act which was signed into law by President Reagan in 1986.[125] The Federal Voting Assistance Program, part of the Department of Defense, was designated to be responsible for administering this Act which was developed for the benefit of U.S. citizens who are active members of the Uniformed Services the Merchant Marine, the commissioned corps of the Public Health Service and the National Oceanic and Atmospheric Administration, and U.S. citizens residing outside the United States. The purpose of the Act was to make it clear the Department of Defense and not the states was responsible to facilitate voting for these three specified classes of eligible voters.

The Department of Defense is responsible for the voting process for eligible voters overseas. The individual states have to send out and count the ballots. In 2014, the states sent 420,094 ballots, roughly half to members of the uniformed services and half to civilians living overseas. Of the ballots sent, only 34.6% (145,509) were returned and submitted for counting.[126] States reported rejecting 8,492, or 5.8%, of the returned ballots. The most common reason given for rejecting these ballots was they were not received on time.

The Military Voter Protection Project is dedicated to promoting and protecting military members' right to vote and ensuring their votes are counted on Election Day. This Project wants military voters to be able to register, request an absentee ballot, and cast a vote regardless of their location in the world. The following described the plight of military voters.

> The challenges faced by military voters are immense. As America's most mobile population, military voters are constantly on the go moving from one duty station to the next. If they have any hope of voting, military voters are required to navigate a confusing array of state absentee voting laws. In many cases, the request for an absentee ballot never comes or comes too late to vote.[127]

The heart of the problem is the process is based on snail mail, ordinary mail delivered by the postal system. The soldier or business person overseas must first send a written request for an absentee ballot. The request must go through the foreign mail service and then through the U.S. mail service to the local election precinct's office. The precinct sends a ballot by the reverse route. When, and if, the ballot gets to the military person, who may have been reassigned to a different location in the meantime, the person must mark his or her vote and then mail it back. According to William Kelleher, PhD, CEO at The Internet Voting Research and Education Fund in Los Angeles,

> Between one fourth and one third of overseas voters are disenfranchised due to land mail problems. Returned ballots, by the time they arrive back home, if they ever do, are usually set aside until the end of the election. Often, absentee ballots are left in a pile on somebody's desk, or stored in a box, and not counted unless they can make a difference in the election. In my opinion, overseas military voters are subjected to a ridiculous and burdensome process of voting.[128]

A Pew Research Survey reported millions of overseas eligible voters did not vote. Sixty percent said that they did not vote because of problems with the absentee voting process.[129] The Survey of 2006 found one-third of all U.S. states do not provide enough time for military personnel stationed overseas to vote and nearly half needed to improve their absentee voting process. Some states required a marked ballot to be notarized, thereby infringing on the voter's right to privacy. The new Act was well intended, but clearly more needs to be done to allow military personnel to be fairly represented in elections.

Voting rights activists viewed the Internet as a possible solution to the deplorable situation of problems with overseas voting. The Clinton administration understood the problem and worked with Congress, which gave the Secretary of Defense the responsibility to develop and fund a pilot program for Americans to vote online. The 2000 pilot project was called Voting Over the Internet. It was the first time the Internet had been used in a general election. In his book *Internet Voting Now: Here's How, Here's Why, So You Can Kiss Citizens United Goodbye!*, Dr. Kelleher reported the outcome of the pilot.

> Four states, Florida, South Carolina, Texas, and Utah participated in the pilot. A website at the Department of Defense provided registration forms and a ballot tailored to each state's regulations. Voters could vote in local, state, and federal races. The Federal Voting Assistance Program submitted an assessment to the Secretary of Defense. There were no problems discovered in the pilot and the technology worked well. The report acknowledged Internet security fears but said they had been mitigated. There were no challenges to the integrity of the Voting over the Internet system.[130]

The project cost six million dollars to design, implement, and test the system before the pilot began. Only 84 votes were cast, as it was intentionally a small pilot. The project directors suggested a larger scale trial be undertaken as the next step. In the Defense Act of 2002, Congress appropriated roughly $30 million and directed the Secretary of Defense to develop a program ultimately capable of handling Internet voting for all six million overseas citizens. The expanded test, which would be for just a fraction of the six million, was to be called the Secure Electronic Registration and Voting Experiment (SERVE) and it would have been conducted by the Federal Voting Assistance Program.

The SERVE project was planned for implementation in the 2004 primary and general elections. It was designed to allow up to 100,000 eligible voters to register to vote in their home precincts and vote remotely using the Internet from anywhere in the world. Arkansas, Florida, Hawaii, North Carolina, South Carolina, Utah, and Washington agreed to participate in the expanded pilot.

The man in charge of the SERVE expanded pilot project was David S. C. Chu, Under Secretary of Defense for Personnel and Readiness. Dr. Kelleher, CEO at The Internet Voting Research and Education Fund in Los Angeles said,

> David Chu and his team felt like they had produced a technological achievement comparable to NASA's Apollo 11 project. Just as the Saturn V rocket put the first man on the moon, so the SERVE technology would carry the first large scale multi-state Internet vote in an actual US election. SERVE was ready for the November 2004 Presidential election.[131]

It was clear there were some risks in using the Internet to vote. However, the Caltech/MIT Voting Technology Project, established by Caltech President David Baltimore and MIT President Charles Vest to prevent a recurrence of the problems that threatened the 2000 U.S. Presidential Election, attempted to support the SERVE expanded pilot project.[132]

In the spirit of transparency, a Security Peer Review Group comprised of 10 members from academia and industry, was established to evaluate the SERVE project and offer a second opinion before the project was approved. The Group had an open invitation to evaluate and comment on any aspect of the SERVE project. Four members of the Group wrote an extremely negative report about the project and recommended it be shut down prior to trying it. The dissenting report said, "There really is no good way to build such a voting system without a radical change in overall architecture of the Internet and the PC, or some unforeseen security break-through."[133] The four dissenters said that the SERVE project was too far ahead of its time, and should be postponed until there is a much improved security infrastructure to build upon.[134] Despite the tens of millions of dollars spent to develop the pilot project with the best possible security and privacy provisions, building upon the success of the smaller pilot, the four dissenters won.

Dr. Kelleher followed the SERVE project closely. With regard to the four dissenters, he said,

> Anything seems possible to these four computer security "specialists" when they assume a sleeping police force, and personal computers with little or no malware or spyware protection. Given these assumptions, they imagine what would happen in our two-party system of election competition. It is possible to imagine widespread attacks that targeted all voters in a particular party for disenfranchisement, leaving the other party unaffected. Such an attack would have serious consequences.[135]

> Yes, it "would" – "would," that is, if all American law enforcement were vacationing in Cancun on Election Day, and everyone was using unprotected PCs. (On the other hand, having the two major parties disenfranchise each other might not be so bad for our country. Independent candidates would win, and perhaps stop the party-driven bickering in Washington.)[136]

On February 6, 2004, Deputy Defense Secretary Paul D. Wolfowitz issued a memorandum ordering Dr. Chu to halt work on the SERVE project. That day was effectively the end of the SERVE project.

After continued problems with the voting process for overseas citizens in the 2004 and 2008 elections, Congress attempted to address the challenges by passing the Military and Overseas Voter Empowerment Act, which was signed into law by President Barack Obama on October 28, 2009. The Act encouraged modernization of absentee voting, but made no mention of Internet technology. The Act required the Department of Defense to create voting assistance offices at every military installation. It urged a robust voter registration system for voters including the ability to update their voter information during the check-in process when they changed duty stations.[137]

This new Act was designed to finally solve the problem of disenfranchised overseas citizens, but the Department of Defense resisted the implementation required to achieve the Act's goals due to resource limitations.[138] Overseas voters were getting weary of the paper based and unreliable process. The absentee ballot data for 2012 painted a bleak picture. While the 2009 Act was intended to increase opportunities to register and request an absentee ballot, the 2012 pre-election data showed a substantial decrease compared to 2008. For example, Virginia, North Carolina, and Ohio saw only 1,746 ballots requested out of the 126,251 military personnel who were eligible.[139]

The National Defense Committee is a War Veterans organization which focuses on veterans affairs and issues important to veterans such as veterans programs, national defense, homeland security, and national security. In 2013, the Committee authored a letter, signed by seventeen computer scientists, urging Congress to allocate Defense Department appropriations for voting research and development. The specific goal was to find practical and secure solutions to enable military members to vote online. Unfortunately, the Committee's effort was squashed by anti-Internet voting activists.

After more than a quarter of a century since President Reagan signed the legislation to improve overseas voting into law, there had not been an increase in the number of military voters. In the FY 2015 National Defense Authorization Act, the long standing requirement for federal voting officials to conduct a remote electronic voting pilot was removed.[140] Veterans, myself included, should be outraged at the lack of support to allow them an easy way to vote and be part of our democracy.

We Can Do Better

In my opinion, the four computer science dissenters to expanding the pilot Internet voting project did military and overseas citizens a great disservice. None of the security threats the dissenters claimed would have occurred with Internet voting have occurred in the elections which have tested Internet voting.[141] I believe the expanded SERVE pilot project likewise would have been successful, just as the first Internet pilot was. The result would have led to the opportunity to vote for millions of Americans.

Instead, the actions of the dissenters resulted in taking away the ability to vote for millions of military and overseas citizens. The dissenters are accountable to no one for this great lost opportunity. For the computer science anti-Internet voting activists to have participated and worked with the Department of Defense to make the pilot a success would have required significant effort on their part. To take down the project was much easier when you have notoriety in the applicable field. I also have a concern about the approach of the dissenters. They declared the Internet as an unacceptable approach to voting without adequately acknowledging the extent of the problems with the current system of paper ballots and antiquated voting machines.

Dave Farber, formerly Chief Technologist at the U.S. Federal Communications Commission who served on the U.S. Presidential Advisory Board on Information Technology, shares a similar view to mine. He is a Trustee of the Electronic Frontier Foundation, a Visiting Professor at the Center for Global Communications at the International University of Japan, and a member of the Verified Voters Board of Advisors. Professor Farber said,

> The dissenting report about the Internet pilot compared the Internet voting system to a perfect system, not to the current system. The latter comparison would have been favorable toward Internet voting. There is nothing we can do to fix the current system. With Internet voting, we can do a lot better.[142]

In *Electronic Elections: The Perils and Promises of Digital Democracy*, Mike Alvarez and Thad Hall also were highly critical of the dissenters. They said, "The dissenters ignored the administrative, political, and legal realities of American elections".[143] Alvarez and Hall gave numerous examples of how the threats and risks the dissenters used to attack the proposed expanded pilot were theoretical and extremely unlikely. They described how the paper and postal service options the military and overseas citizens were left with were even more subject to error than Internet voting.

Mail Votes Lost or Not Counted

Some people lose their ballot or mail it too late for it to be counted. The pipeline from deciding to vote to having a vote actually counted can be long and frustrating. Charles Stewart III, the Kenan Sahin Distinguished Professor of Political Science at MIT, studied the question of whether voting by mail causes more lost votes, compared to in-person voting. In a published study, "Losing Votes by Mail", Stewart concluded, "The number of lost votes through the Vote By Mail system in 2008 may have been as large as 7.6 million."[144] The number represents approximately one in five citizens who attempted to vote by mail. These votes include voters at home and abroad. The 7.6 million lost votes included 3.9 million absentee ballots requested but never received, 2.9 million ballots received but not returned, and .8 million returned but not counted.

The ballots received but not returned can be due to a ballot lost in the mail or the voter deciding to vote at the polls or not vote at all. Votes returned but not counted can be a result of numerous kinds of errors. Typical errors include the ballot envelope not being signed, the name not matching the voter registration list, failure to provide the voter's address, missing or bad signatures, no witness signature (if required), no ballot application on record, missed deadline, already voted in person, or the voter had died.

Stewart acknowledged criticism of his study.[145] The vote by mail process is more complicated than the study's assumptions. There could be some errors in his data. If Stewart's study result of 7.6 million lost votes was wrong by half, the result would still show 10% of the 2008 mail in votes were lost. If 10% of voters who voted at the polls were not able to complete their vote, there would have been outrage.

Voter Fraud

The purported frequency and extent of voter fraud is a highly controversial issue. There can be no question there is a perception of voter fraud. Vivid stories have been passed through generations. One of the most famous is a reported quote from Earl Long (1895-1960), Governor of Louisiana. "When I die, if I die, I want to be buried in Louisiana, so I can stay active in politics."[146] Losing candidates often contribute to the lore.[147] The facts however, do not demonstrate voter fraud. In 2012, Loyola law professor Justin Levitt estimated, "Over the previous twelve years, the voting fraud rate was 0.000002%."[148] He found only nine instances of specific allegations of voter fraud out of approximately 400 million voters. Voter fraud was used as the reason for Governor Scott Walker's determination to make the special voter id requirements in Wisconsin more stringent and difficult. Even though a 2014 study at Marquette University found 39 percent of voters from a Wisconsin state-wide poll believed voter fraud affected a few thousand votes at each election, no claims of voter fraud were substantiated.[149]

In *Deliver the Vote*, author and political historian Tracy Campbell said, "A persistent culture of corruption has long thrived in American elections." He studied records from hundreds of elections from pre-colonial days through the 2004 election. Electoral fraud had many varieties.

It also can happen when a person submits ballots in multiple voting booths. A ballot stuffer could vote on behalf of people who did not appear at the polls, were dead, or were fictitious characters. Campbell's research concluded electoral fraud was not confined to one party, location, or time period.[150] It is hard to garner specific fraud numbers from Campbell's book. Kevin Pallister, Lecturer of Political Science at University of Massachusetts-Amherst said, "Campbell includes voter suppression under his broad label of 'election fraud'. His book should not be taken as support for contemporary charges that voter fraud is rampant."[151]

Some politicians have alleged voter fraud is rampant and is jeopardizing the integrity of American elections and democracy. The allegations claim elections are being stolen by unscrupulous registration activists, vote buyers, and illegal immigrants voting. Despite a history of stories about fraud, I found no contemporary charges voter fraud is rampant. In *The Myth of Voter Fraud*, Lorraine C. Minnite describes the results of her research to find evidence of voter fraud. She contended that while voting irregularities created by our complex and fragmented electoral process in the United States are common, intentional voter fraud is quite rare. Minnite examined public records obtained from all fifty state governments and the U.S. Department of Justice. She concluded, "Voter fraud is in reality a politically constructed myth intended to further complicate the voting process and reduce voter turnout."[152] Another aspect of voting relates to where you vote.

Priming

Ben Pryor, a researcher at Oklahoma State University, believes America should eliminate voting at traditional voting places. The premise of Pryor's argument revolves around priming. Priming is a method by which a polling location can influence a voter's opinion and consequently how they vote. Priming can arise through one's subconscious memory based on a perceived relationship between objects and ideas. For example, a vote to increase the school budget may get more supportive votes from a polling place in a local school rather than voting at a church or other location. A vote about marriage may get different support at a church polling place than at a school. Pryor cited numerous studies by social science researchers confirming statistically significant differences in outcomes based on the actual type of polling place. His conclusion, published in the *New Republic*, is, "The time is right to end in-person voting and adopt voting my mail".[153]

Weather

Even with an adequate number of polling places and a sufficient quantity of the correct kind of ballots on hand, other problems can affect voter participation. Long lines in bad weather can dissuade voters, especially the elderly or people with special needs, from voting. Some polling places make voters wait outside since they can only accommodate a small number of voters inside. A friend told me that her sister in Wisconsin waited outside in 40 degree weather and high winds for an hour and 45 minutes to vote. Her son in Florida had to wait outside five hours in the sun. Work schedules can make it impossible for some workers to get adequate time to drive in bad weather to and from the voting location. Inadequate, convenient parking can prevent some people from voting particularly in hazardous weather. In some polling places, there is insufficient, designated handicapped parking.

People with Special Needs

Some voters may be ill and homebound on Election Day. Other voters may not try to vote because their disabilities may impose physical limitations in using the voting equipment. There are at least 35 million voting-age people with disabilities in the United States, representing 1 out of 7 voting-age people. This number is likely to grow with the aging of the population. People with disabilities have lower voter turnout than people without disabilities. Lisa Schur, Associate Professor at Rutgers University, said, "Twelve surveys covering the 1992-2004 elections, using varying samples and definitions of disability, found eligible citizens with disabilities were between 4 and 21 percent less likely to vote than eligible citizens without disabilities." The lower voter turnout among people with disabilities appears to be caused in part by their greater likelihood of experiencing voting difficulties.

Ted Selker, Ph.D., Visiting Scientist, Center for Information Technology in Interest of Society at UC Berkeley and Fellow of the Institute of Electrical and Electronic Engineers, has been intrigued by how to decrease the polling place challenges facing voters with vision, hearing, and other disabilities. When he was MIT

Director of the Caltech/MIT Voting Technology Project, Dr. Selker built and tested technology for improving voting security and accuracy, with special attention to the needs of impaired voters.[154] As the inventor of the TrackPoint for the IBM ThinkPad, Dr. Selker has significant experience at inventing technology to enhance the user experience with technology. One of his inventions used audio technology to recite to a voter with a disability what choice he or she had made.

Conclusion

The problems with existing voting systems are challenging. The Federal Government provided funding for new voting machines in 2002, but did not provide funding to maintain or replace them when they became out dated. Unfortunately, the machines are at the end of their life cycle, in fact at a crisis. One alternative to resolve the problem is to patch the existing system of antiquated machines. Another alternative is to embrace an election attitude.

An election attitude offers a practical approach to voting. A key component of the new attitude is Internet voting. It uses mobile devices and the Internet to enable citizens to vote from the comfort and privacy of their home or at a local library. Though the risks are real and cannot be ignored, there are numerous benefits to adopting Internet voting. With Internet voting it can replicate successful web services such as Amazon which is used by millions of people daily. If voting online could reach the level of adoption of e-commerce, it would be possible for voter participation to increase significantly. With a changed focus, increased funding, changes in election registration and security, and increased access for people with special needs, I believe the voter participation rate would be improved. The focus of the next chapter is Internet voting, a visionary approach to voting based on a new election attitude.

CHAPTER 3

A Better Way to Vote

T he American voting system faces major problems. I believe these problems deserve immediate attention. One solution is to spend billions of dollars on updated voting machines and hope manufacturers can make them more reliable and secure. A better alternative is for federal, state, and local election officials, voting technology vendors, and citizens to adopt an election attitude.

Election Attitude for All

An election attitude is a different way of thinking about the voting process. For election officials and voting technology vendors, an election attitude means putting the citizens first, making it easy to register and vote in a way which provides the security, privacy, accuracy, verifiability, auditability, and reliability people expect. While there are differences between Internet voting and e-commerce, there also is an analogy which I described in my book, *Net Attitude: What It Is, How to Get It, and Why You Need It More Than Ever* (2015). I described in detail how Amazon has a net attitude which makes shopping and buying easy and satisfies customers.

Try to imagine e-commerce operating without a net attitude. For example, you want to buy something from a website. The website company sends you a letter with a password so you can login. After you find the item you want to buy, you click on it, and the website says, "Click here to request a printed catalog, and click here for the name and location of the nearest dealer who carries our product." You enter your zip code and look at the list of dealers. You find the nearest dealer and click on their link. The website says, "Please call us Monday to Friday between 9 AM and 5 PM." The scenario I just described is the way it was for most retail e-commerce sites in the mid 1990s. Some e-commerce sites are still difficult to use.[155] A buyer's priority is to get the product they want. Some companies have websites to describe their products, but their priority is to protect their dealers. Putting the buyer in second place is not a net attitude.

The Internet was not always convenient. I can remember my first attempts at connecting to the Internet in 1993. Getting connected required extensive technical steps. Once connected, there was a good chance you would be disconnected shortly. When connected, the Internet was slow and there was not much you could do other than look at files and documents. The enormous improvement in reliability and capabilities between then and now did not occur overnight. There were many steps along the way.

The structuring and formatting of content for a web page was done using hypertext markup language (HTML). HTML version 1 was introduced in 1992. In 1993, there was only one web browser available to view HTML content. It was called Mosaic. It was followed in 1994-95 by Netscape, Opera, and Internet Explorer. Safari, Chrome, and Firefox were introduced between 2003 and 2008. The World Wide Web Consortium continuously developed enhancements to HTML with increasingly powerful capabilities for formatting of a document. There was no audio and no video on the web in its infancy. In the late 1990s, cascading style sheets were introduced and offered the capability to format a web page so it would look appropriate whether on a big desktop display, a small handheld display, or a tablet.

Between the late 1990s and 2008, there were many incremental improvements to how webpages could be designed and browsed. In 2008, HTML 5 enabled developers to create complex web applications which worked on any kind of device. In 2011, Content Security Policy for the web was introduced to prevent some of the severe web based attacks against users and websites. These are just a few of the key steps of web development. Although the web is continuously evolving, the Internet by itself is insecure. However, by utilizing various protocols, tools, and techniques government, businesses, and consumers have found the Internet to be adequate for their uses. The Internet has evolved from a government and academic file sharing and messaging system to a global network which touches every aspect of our lives. One example of this is e-commerce.

Amazon began selling books online in 1995. Books were the only thing Amazon sold, but founder Jeff Bezos had a vision for the company to become "an everything store".[156]Amazon expanded its offerings with a string of investments and acquisitions including Pets.com (1999), CDnow.com (2003), Smallparts.com, an industrial component supplier (2005), Shopbop, a retailer of designer clothing and accessories for women (2006), Audible.com (2008), and shoe and clothing retailer Zappos.com (2009). Between 1995 and 2015, the company made more than 50 acquisitions or significant investments.[157] Mr. Bezos followed the mantra I described in *Net Attitude*, "Think Big, Act Bold, Start Simple, Iterate Fast".[158] "Think Big", become an everything store. "Act Bold", make strategic investments and disrupt existing business models. "Start Simple", sell just books. "Iterate Fast", continuously innovate and acquire companies with good ideas.

Amazon's formula has worked. By 2015, Amazon sold over 480 million products in the USA across dozens of departments including over 30 million items in the combined Clothing, Shoes & Jewelry department, 24 million in Sports & Outdoors, 60 million in Home & Kitchen, and 96 million in Electronics.[159] [160] In 2014, Amazon sold 63% of all books bought online and 40% of all books sold overall. Amazon's revenue for 2015 was $107 billion and it was the fastest rate any company reached $100 billion in annual sales.[161] One of the factors behind the explosive growth at Amazon has been customer service.

Let's explore a situation where you have a problem with an order you placed at Amazon. The website has extensive and easy to request solutions, but suppose none of the solutions exactly matches your problem. You want to communicate directly. A couple of clicks and you are presented with a choice of E-mail, Phone, or Live Chat. You select Phone and enter your phone number. You then receive a choice of Call Me Now or Call Me in 5 Minutes. You click Call Me Now, your phone rings and you are connected to a customer service associate. They solve your problem and your issue is resolved. This quick process represents a company with a net attitude.

Federal, state, and local election officials, and voting technology vendors could adopt an election attitude. Some officials are working on making changes, creating a voting system which makes it easy for citizens to register and vote in a way they trust because it provides the security, privacy, verifiability, and auditability they expect.

An election attitude for citizens is equally important for a strong democracy. Citizens with an election attitude take voting seriously and give voting a high priority. They inform themselves about the issues and candidates on which they will be voting. Citizens with an election attitude register to vote and keep their registration information current. When election day arrives, they vote and feel satisfied they have done their part to make their voice heard.

More Than Convenience

Voting remotely via the Internet can have a number of advantages in addition to convenience. Dr. Selker told me that too many people often go to a polling place unprepared. It is illegal to canvas at a polling place, so many have no way to learn about their choices at the time they are making selections. He said, "The remote place you vote from may be the place where you can explore and learn about the race you are making a selection on while you are making it."[162]

For those overseas, remote voting can mean enfranchisement not easily provided by the absentee ballot process. For people with disabilities, there can be multiple new solutions to ease or eliminate barriers. A voter could use a handheld device such as a smartphone or tablet. They could use voice activated or dictation apps to express their vote. Voters could reflect on their voting decision without the pressure to get back to work or rush to pick up kids from school or get to a doctor appointment. Faster compilation of election results by eliminating paper, faxes, and outdated manual procedures can increase confidence of voters that their votes were counted quickly and accurately. When results are delayed by hours and sometimes more than a day, voters justifiably can question what is wrong with the voting process.

An election attitude includes convenience with a capital C because we are a convenience based society. We can shop, compare, buy, search, learn, and manage our health using the Internet. Previously, the Internet was only available on a desktop computer. Today, the Internet is wherever we are, including on our wrists or in our eye glasses. Mobile technology has enhanced convenience in many areas. However, in most situations, the election process is not convenient. Those who have stood in line in bad weather for hours would say it is very inconvenient.

Retail e-commerce has grown at double digit rates from 1995, when Amazon began, to $340 billion in the U.S. for 2015.[163] Use of the web in other aspects of the economy also grew dramatically. In the 1980s, the IRS recognized efficient tax collection was becoming more difficult. Converting paper returns into machine readable data was a complex, time-consuming, and error-prone process. In 1986, a pilot of electronic filing began with 5 tax preparers in 3 cities. Twenty-five thousand returns were filed.[164] Tax preparers found the process productive and quickly expanded e-file use. Once consumer programs such as TurboTax were commercially available and supported e-file, its use facilitated quick returns. When the IRS encouraged e-filing, it grew even faster. In 2011, a milestone of one billion electronically filed returns was achieved. In 2015, more than 128 million tax returns, representing 91% of all return, were filed using E-filing.[165] The IRS said, "Using the Internet is the fastest and most accurate way to file individual and business tax returns".[166]

E-filing has not been without its problems. In early 2016, the IRS identified and halted an automated attack upon its Electronic Filing PIN application on IRS.gov. Using social security numbers stolen from outside the IRS, identity thieves used malware in an attempt to generate E-file PINs which could potentially be used to electronically file a tax return. No personal taxpayer data was compromised or disclosed by IRS systems, but approximately 100,000 of the stolen social security numbers were used to successfully access an E-file PIN.[167] The number of accesses was less than one tenth of one percent of tax returns filed in 2015. The IRS is continually reviewing and improving security of its servers.

Between 2000 and 2013, numerous Internet services have been started and millions of consumers trust them with their private information. The following is a sample listed in order of their founding: TripAdvisor, Wikipedia, LinkedIn, Skype, Facebook, YouTube, Twitter, Tumblr, Dropbox, Kickstarter, Instagram, Pinterest, Snapchat, and Coursera. The diversity of types of services and the ever increasing number of users demonstrates consumers trust using the Internet.

A 2016 J.D. Power Study of Consumer Banking confirmed the continued growth of Internet banking.[168] 80% of customers are satisfied with Internet banking. However, satisfaction with mobile Internet banking is above 85%. The use of ATMs and Internet banking is causing the number of physical bank branches to decline while the percentage of people opening accounts online is increasing.[169]

While business to consumer e-commerce in companies such as Amazon was growing, businesses were increasing their trust in using the Internet for non-consumer e-business. Business to business e-commerce in the U.S. grew to $780 billion and represented 9.3 percent of all sales of this type by the end of 2015.[170] According to research provider Frost & Sullivan, global e-commerce between businesses will be twice as large as retail e-commerce by 2020, growing to $6.7 trillion vs. $3.2 trillion.[171]

Public companies are another important segment of the American economy which are dependent on the Internet. They use the Internet for shareholder voting. By the end of 2015, there were 3,700 publicly traded companies.[172] Shareholders of these companies vote their shares at annual meetings or when a special vote may be needed. Most shareholders do not attend shareholder meetings. They vote by proxy. In effect, shareholders give their voting preference to an investment firm which holds their shares or they give their proxy vote directly to the company in which they own shares. Prior to the Internet, proxy voting was handled by mail. Today, Broadridge Financial Solutions, Inc., a Lake Success, New York based public company operates an Internet based e-proxy service called proxyvoting.com.

In 2015, Broadridge facilitated the proxy voting for 4,114 shareholder meetings. This Internet based service processed the votes of 455 billion shares, representing approximately 95% of all shares voted.[173] The remaining 5% were voted by paper ballots. Shareholders vote to approve the company's audit firm, elect members of their Board of Directors, change company policy on business and societal issues, mergers, acquisitions, and other issues. Due to the critical importance of many of the issues brought to a vote by publicly owned companies, security is of the utmost importance.

Broadridge operates secure Internet servers. Each ballot cast is assigned a unique 16 digit control number so votes can be verified and audited. The company uses an independent auditor to verify random selections of votes. When large blocks of stock are voted, for example 50,000 shares, the vote is audited three times to confirm the owner of the shares is correct. In addition to providing a secure and verifiable election process using the Internet, Broadridge's technologies and processing saved corporate users an estimated $1 billion in the 2015 proxy season compared to what would have been spent had the companies used traditional printing and mailing.[174]

Another rapidly growing area of Internet usage is in non-cash payments. A joint venture between the consulting firm Capgemini and The Royal Bank of Scotland produced the 2015 World Payments Report. This Report showed there were 358 billion non-cash payments in 2013, the latest year for which official market data is available.[175] Non-cash payments include payments made with instruments other than notes and coins. This includes credit transfers, direct debits, credit or debit cards, and checks. In 2000, checks were used in more than 40 billion transactions, but the number was down to less than 20 billion in October 2012.[176] The data is not available for 2015, but based on trends, I believe checks likely represented less than 5% of non-cash payments. The growth in non-cash payments is coming from e-commerce, online banking, payment transfer services such as PayPal and Xoom, and generally wider use of the Internet for financial transactions. Mobile payments through services such as Apple Pay, are relatively small but growing rapidly. Forrester Research estimated 2014 in-person mobile payments at $3.7 billion and growing to $34 billion by 2019.[177] The authors of the World Payments Report said, "Customers expect the ease of use and immediacy they experience with the Internet."[178]

The Report also highlighted the transformation underway in how money is transferred. Many nations across the globe have implemented Internet payment security measures. The Reserve Bank of India mandated two-factor authentication for all online credit card payments. In this system, an online user must enter login and password credentials plus a numeric security code sent to the user's mobile phone. Providing security for financial transactions requires continuous innovation and transformation of payment processing. The Report said, "Offerings based upon immediate payments systems and new technologies such as blockchain will increasingly be the route via which customer demands are met."[179]

Dependence on the Internet is evident in many aspects of American everyday life beyond financial transactions and e-commerce. As of 2015, SurveyMonkey had 25 million users.[180] Employees at 99% of the Fortune 500 have used SurveyMonkey online surveys. The users provided 90 million survey responses a month.[181]

Another example of a high level of Internet use is by Kaiser Permanente, a healthcare giant in California. This company is a pioneer in leveraging the Internet, using patient portals, to engage 45 percent of its 9.5 million members for patient communications.[182] Kaiser's online portals provide secure physician-patient email and access to a comprehensive electronic health record system. In 2015, 72% of Internet users obtained health-related information online.[183]

The trends are clear. Consumers and businesses are trusting the Internet with billions of dollars, billions of transactions, and the voting of billions of shares of publicly traded companies. Consumers and hospitals are trusting the Internet with sensitive personal medical information. Americans recognize the security of the Internet is not perfect, but they recognize procedures and technology continue to improve. They don't compare the Internet to a perfect world, they compare it to a world of paper, faxes, delays, and inaccuracies with legacy processes. There is considerable debate among experts about whether Internet security is getting better or worse.[184] Considering all aspects of how we use the Internet, I believe security is getting better. More people are doing more things with increased convenience and positive results. An election attitude can bring the same kind of positive thinking to the voting process.

CHAPTER 4

Voting Innovation

S ince we use outdated and unreliable voting equipment, the average voter might ask, "Why can't we vote on the Internet? We do everything else on the Internet, why can't we vote there?" I wish I could respond widespread Internet voting is coming soon. It is not likely, but it would come more quickly if a positive election attitude was adopted.

In this chapter, I describe a brief history of Internet voting trials including Internet voting in other countries. I also will outline the challenges to Internet voting. The current voting system needs considerable innovation to modernize it. I will highlight some distinctive examples of progress in modernization of voting in six key areas.

1) Progress with Internet voting in specific voting jurisdictions including Estonia, Arizona, Michigan, Utah, and Los Angeles, California. I will discuss a project in Travis County, Texas which is innovative but excludes the Internet.

2) A review of states which have adopted methods of transmitting ballots over the Internet. It is not specifically Internet voting, but a step in the right direction.

3) The voting machine industry and how it responds to the need for improved voting systems. The discussion will include the emergence of newcomers to the industry who may threaten the voting machine industry status quo. I will highlight accomplishments of some of the new voting technology companies.

4) What the Open Source Elections Technology Foundation is doing to make voting more secure and reliable.

5) Blockchain technology, the technology infrastructure which underlies digital currencies such as Bitcoin. Blockchain technology may be the ultimate solution to enable an election attitude to emerge.

6) Smartphones, how they have become an important part of our lives, and could have the potential to be the ideal tool for voting.

Estonia

The Republic of Estonia is widely recognized as a pioneer in Internet voting since it is the only country in the world to offer Internet voting to all of its citizens. Estonia borders Russia to the east and Latvia to the south. Helsinki, Finland is 53 miles to the north across the Baltic Sea and Stockholm, Sweden is 233 miles to the west of Tallinn, the capital of Estonia. The population of Estonia is 1.3 million, slightly larger than Dallas, Texas.[185]

Estonia began working on using the Internet to vote, which they call I-voting, in 2002. The original online voting system was created especially for the National Election Committee. The development spanned three years and was done in partnership with an Estonian information and communications technology company called Cybernetica AS. I-voting was first used in the local elections of 2005. Traditional voting at polling places was and continues to be available. In 2005, nine thousand voters cast their ballot via the Internet.[186] This represented two percent of all participating voters.

Since 2005, Internet voting has been carried out eight times in local elections in October 2005, October 2009 and October 2013, Parliamentary elections in March 2007, March 2011 and March 2015 and European Parliament elections in June 2009 and May 2014.

Estonia's Internet voting has seen steady growth. In the Parliamentary elections in 2007, 30,000 voters, five percent of the participating voters, used I-voting.[187] In the European Parliament elections in 2009 the numbers nearly doubled to 58,000, or 15 per cent. In the local elections of October 2009, I-voting was offered for the fourth time. Voting at a polling place continued to be an option, but voting via the Internet continued to grow. The I-voting numbers rose to 104,000, 16 percent. In the Parliamentary elections of 2015, more than 176,000 used I-voting representing 31% of all voters.[188]

The approach Estonia has taken to implement Internet voting is to emulate an absentee ballot by mail process.[189] These are the typical steps in absentee voting.

✓ A voter presents an ID document to be identified.
✓ The voter receives a ballot and two envelopes.
✓ The voter casts their vote on the ballot and puts it in the envelope. The envelope has no information about the identity of the voter.
✓ The voter encloses the sealed envelope with the ballot into an outer envelope on which the voter's information is written.
✓ The envelope is delivered to the voter's polling place by the postal service.
✓ The polling place confirms the eligibility of the voter and opens the outer envelope.
✓ The anonymous inner envelope is put in the ballot box.

The Estonian voting system goes well beyond the two-envelope system. The following are the steps, as explained to me by Mr. Anto Veldre, previously an information security expert at the Computer Emergency Response Team of the Estonian Information System Authority.

✓ The voter goes to the Election Committee secure website and downloads a voting app.
✓ The voter is identified and authenticated by inserting a secure chip ID card, which was issued by the Estonian government., into an inexpensive reader which can be purchased locally and attached to a personal computer. All Estonian citizens have a unique ID card. A PIN is required for use with the chip ID card. Citizens who do not want to vote this way can go to polling places in person.
✓ The voting precinct is determined based on the voter registration data. The appropriate candidate list for the voter is securely downloaded and displayed on the voter's computer.
✓ The app downloaded from the Estonia government is used to encrypt the vote. This is the equivalent of the internal envelope.
✓ The app is used to sign the vote. This is the equivalent of the outer envelope.
✓ The remaining steps are performed after the polls have closed by the election officials.

✓ The digital outer envelopes are separated and a list is prepared by the election officials of the voters who participated.

✓ If more than one envelope is discovered for the same voter, only the latest one will be counted. This is an important step to prevent coercion. If someone coerces a voter to cast a certain vote, he or she can later vote again. The last vote counts.

✓ The list of voters is compared to the list of people who voted in person at the polls. If a person voted online and in person, only the in person vote is counted. This would not be typical, but it could happen. If a person has second thoughts, and wants to vote in person, they can do so.

✓ The digital inner envelopes are decrypted. The secret key used to decrypt the envelopes is hidden up to this point so the ballot cannot be stolen.

✓ The decrypted ballots, showing the candidate IDs, are summed to produce the final election result for the online voters.

Despite the fact Estonia has not experienced any voter fraud or security problems affecting the outcome of the vote, there are Internet voting skeptics. Also in America, some anti-Internet activists do not support using the Internet for voting. Although Estonia has implemented procedural safeguards, some American anti-Internet activists are concerned about whether or not it is possible to have adequate security and privacy provisions in any voting system which uses personal computers and the Internet.

A common theme of opponents to Internet voting is security. Harri Hursti, an independent researcher from Finland who works for the web security company SafelyLocked reviewed Internet voting in Estonia and said, "These computers could have easily been compromised by criminals or foreign hackers, undermining the security of the whole system."[190] The Estonian National Electoral Committee said that it took any evidence of flaws in balloting seriously, but in the past decade its online balloting had stood up to numerous reviews and security tests. The Election Committee said, "We believe that online balloting allows us to achieve a level of security greater than what is possible with paper ballots."[191] In effect, those opposed to Internet voting say that if your voting system uses the Internet to cast ballots, it should be shut down, as was their recommendation for Estonia. Estonia, in effect said that Internet voting is not perfect, but it is better than voting using the old methods of ballots, scanners, touch screens, and voting machines with old and unreliable technology.

Anti-Internet voting activists have a strong belief the Internet should not be used for voting. They have written papers, given speeches, testified, and conducted tests to demonstrate their concerns. In 2014, a group of disbelieving anti-Internet voting activists from the University of Michigan visited Estonia to evaluate there Internet-based I-voting system. The group published their findings at estoniaevoting.org.[192] Since Estonia is the only country in the world which significantly relied on Internet voting for national elections, the anti-Internet voting activists wanted to study the strengths and weaknesses and share the results of their analysis with the world's technologists and decision makers. The researchers studied the system by observing Estonia's I-voting during their 2013 municipal elections. They analyzed documents, software, and conducted experiments on voting servers they recreated in a laboratory setting.

The first conclusion of the researchers was the security architecture of the voting system is not adequate to withstand state level cyberattacks such as those experienced by China against U.S. companies or the U.S. against Iran. They highlighted theoretical risks in which sophisticated attackers could change votes or even disrupt an election. The researchers highlighted gaps in operational security and procedures which they believed could leave the system open to attack and manipulation. They constructed a clone of the I-voting system in a laboratory and used computer science techniques to attack it. Mr. Veldre pointed out Estonia had its servers protected by extra layers of organizational and procedural measures. The researchers however, had physical access to the cloned servers in their own laboratory and were free to infect the servers with any malware they considered necessary. Such direct access to physical servers would be highly improbable for hackers.

They were able to introduce malware and software bots which could rig the vote count. They demonstrated a theoretical attack which could be replicated across tens of thousands of voters' computers. The experiments were simplified by ignoring some difficult to replicate items such as the Estonian National ID chip card ecosystem and the hardware security module technology Estonia used to decrypt ballots.

The researchers acknowledged Estonia's efforts to provide transparency to the technology behind the voting system, but they did not find them sufficiently compelling to instill confidence in the system. The researchers took it upon themselves to recommend Estonian I-voting be discontinued immediately.[193] There was no acknowledgement of the shortcomings and risks of paper based voting systems.

The Estonian Electoral Committee and the Estonian Information Authority were concerned about American computer science visitors declaring the government I-voting system unfit. Anto Veldre, made a vigorous response to the estoniaevoting.org findings. In an article titled, "E-voting is (too) secure".[194] The article was in Estonian, but due to significant interest around the world, the article was translated into English. Mr. Veldre said, "The researchers were more interested in making a public display of errors they found than assisting Estonia in identifying the details of what they found so they could be fixed expeditiously."[195] In response to the researcher's allegation that voter PCs may have been infected with malware, Mr. Veldre told me, "This was an acknowledged risk".[196] He further pointed out, "Any voter concerned about their PC could go to vote at the regular polling place."[197] Another serious allegation of the American researchers was the DVDs from which the e-voting systems was installed could have been infected. In response, Mr. Veldre said,

> This is a valid claim, THEORETICALLY. Just like a storm hitting Estonia on the day of the elections and paralyzing our energy system, the explosion of a neutron bomb on a train arriving at the Main Railway Station or the Sun transforming into a Supernova.[198]

His point was a DVD used by the technical staff could be infected, but it was highly unlikely. One of the most important challenges of Internet voting is how to confirm a voter's identity. The Police and Border Guard Board of Estonia facilitated voter identification by issuing plastic ID cards to all citizens. A person in Estonia had to appear in person to get their card. Once they had a card, they could use it for identification purposes for themselves from home or work. The authentication is done by inserting their card into a personal computer reader where they enter a PIN, just like most American credit cards now require with chip cards.

Estonia has a nationally supported Public Key Infrastructure which issues digital identities to Estonian citizens. The chip card IDs make it possible to remotely identify cardholders. In addition to supporting the I-voting system, the Public Key Infrastructure can be used by Estonian banks, the Tax Board, and company websites. Having a centralized system for remote authentication and digital signing is a major advantage for Estonia. Estonian legislation backs up the validity of the system. The national infrastructure Estonia has created for empowering citizens with digital IDs is something many countries, including the United States, have talked about, but Estonia actually made it real for its citizens.

The National Electoral Committee of Estonia commissioned a study of the issues and security risks inherent in the I-voting system. Nine experts collaborated on the original study, and it was then updated in 2010.[199] The study team evaluated the general suitability of the security provisions in the I-voting plan. They thoroughly mapped the technical and organizational risks of the system and made recommendations for improvement where they felt it was necessary. Although the system they had was working, the Estonian government wanted to continually review and improve their processes. Estonia was confident in I-voting from the start, but it is committed to continue making it better.

While Mr. Veldre would acknowledge the I-voting system of Estonia is not perfect, he explained in his article, "Estonians' experience of integrity problems with the paper based system made them confident in the Internet voting system". He continued, "During the Soviet era, the Communist Party always received 97-99% of votes in all polling stations. There were very real memories of the practices used to falsify the paper based voting system the researchers urged the country to rely on".[200] The current President of Estonia, Toomas Hendrik Ilves, is very supportive of Internet voting. He said, "It's rather difficult to bribe a computer."[201]

Mr. Veldre believes, despite the risks and imperfection of personal computer hardware and software, it is still possible to create systems to compensate for the security exposures. "We can build software and procedures on top of these systems that are owned by the state of Estonia and use the Internet as the communications channel. Every movement that is important for the outcome (of the voting process) is logged and the e-voting process is observed by dozens of information technology people."[202]

I believe the American anti-Internet voting activists found actual risks which can and probably have been corrected by the Estonian I-voting system. The anti-Internet voting activists identified some theoretical risks to the integrity and security of the I-voting system. Security is not perfect in any information technology system. Paper based systems are not perfect either. I think the Estonian Internet voting innovation is commendable. It appears their risk assessment, monitoring, and software development processes are working. Estonia has conducted I-voting eight times without security incidents.

Other European Internet Voting

The U.S. Election Assistance Commission published "A Survey of Internet Voting" in 2011. The survey highlighted 12 countries in Europe which used or piloted Internet voting in some form since 2000. The results were mixed, but some of the countries believed their Internet voting trials were successful. Verified Voting, a Carlsbad, CA advocacy group for auditable voting, but strongly opposed to Internet voting, said, "This may be due to an abundance of optimism about the challenge of securing such elections."[203] The Verified Voting comments continue a pattern of comparing Internet voting projects to perfection instead of comparing them to the existing problem filled voting systems.

Some European countries have legislation which bans Internet voting for national elections. Some of the pilots were restricted to local elections or elections in educational systems. One country making considerable progress in use of the Internet in voting is Switzerland. Since 2004 at the federal level, the country has conducted more than 150 online voting trials. Even more were conducted at the local level. During the 2013 federal election, 58% of overseas Swiss citizens voted online.[204] The Swiss government has allocated funds for continued enhancement of Internet voting technology, and has set a goal of providing an online voting option for all voters in the near future.[205]

Estonia remains as the only country in Europe to have continuously conducted national elections using Internet voting. The U.S. trials also have had mixed results, like Europe. The following sections will describe some of the more successful pilots.

Arizona Primary (2000)

On March 27, 2001, Daniel Rubin submitted his Bachelor of Science in Computer Science thesis to the School of Engineering and Applied Science faculty at the University of Virginia. The title was "The Security of Remote Online Voting". In the thesis, Rubin said, "March 7 (2000) began a new era for American elections. Registered Democrats in Arizona could cast legally-binding ballots through the Internet for their Presidential primary choice from anywhere in the world."[206]

The Democratic Party of Arizona hired election.com, an Internet startup company, to administer the voting system for the 2000 Democratic primary election. Registered voters had to express interest in voting via the Internet by January 24, 2000 to be eligible to vote in the March election. Arizonans interested in voting using the Internet could register on the Internet. The voter was sent a PIN for use in the voting process. Voting could be done from the voter's computer between March 7 and March 11, prior to Election Day. The U.S. Election Assistance Commission reported, "Problems experienced while using the voting system on voter PCs during the election included: malfunction of antiquated browsers, operating system incompatibility, issues such as a voter losing the PIN required for accessing the voting system."[207] Election.com and the election officials declared the 2000 Democratic primary Internet voting a success.

The 2000 turnout in the Presidential primary was barely 10% of registered Democrats. The Internet votes accounted for 46% of the votes cast. The key factor behind the six-fold turnout boost was young voters. Rubin said, "Of the Internet votes cast in Arizona, 75 percent of them were from people between 18 and 24 years old. During the 1996 Presidential election, less than one-third of the people between ages 18 and 24 voted."[208]

The biggest blemish on the 2000 Democratic primary election arose from a suit filed by the Voting Integrity Project, a nonpartisan, nonprofit group based in Virginia. The group sued the Arizona Democratic Party for discriminating against poor and minority voters. They argued lack of Internet capability would disenfranchise the minority voters. The group attempted to block the 2000 Internet voting. Even though Attorney General Janet Reno vetted the Arizona primary for compliance with the 1965 Voting Rights Act, the Voting Integrity Project argued, "Poor and minority voters are statistically less likely to be wired than white and Asian citizens"[209] A federal judge allowed the Democrats to proceed with the 2000 Internet election. Voters could still go to the polling places. No voter was required to vote via the Internet. If someone wanted to vote online but had no computer, they could visit a local library and vote from there.

The 2000 Democratic primary election with Internet voting proved to be a success. Approximately 37,000 Arizona Democrats voted online in the primary.[210] Many were able to vote from countries all over the world. Another 20,000 voted by mail, with 20,000 others physically voting at polling stations. Turnout was twice as large as in any other Arizona Democratic primary since 1984. Deborah Phillips, President of the Voting Integrity Project, warned of hackers, voter fraud, loss of privacy, and lack of access for some communities. Although there was criticism from voting and technical experts, there was no report of privacy or security issues.[211]

Daniel Rubin summed it up well.

Experts need to be more open to the fact that someday, Internet voting will be a reality. Being critical of our current, premature schemes and protocols is fine; do not write off the technology just yet. They should work to fix the problems rather than criticize them.[212]

Florida (2000)

Florida has been active in the voting arena for nearly two decades. The state has a large military population and the decision to not continue with the expanded pilot for military and overseas citizens to vote using the Internet was a great disappointment. I spoke to Paul Lux, Okaloosa County Supervisor of Elections about voting. Okaloosa County is home to various units of all five branches of the military including Eglin Air Force Base near Valparaiso, Florida. The county has 128,000 registered voters and more than 25,000 are military voters.[213] At election time, 3,000 or more military voters are overseas or otherwise out of the county.[214]

As discussed in chapter 2, Florida, South Carolina, Texas, and Utah were the four states which participated in the 2000 pilot of Internet voting for the military and overseas citizens. Of the votes cast during the pilot, approximately half were from Okaloosa registered voters. The pilot was successful and Okaloosa County volunteered to be part of the expanded pilot which was to take place in 2004. Unfortunately, the expanded pilot was cancelled after dissenting anti-Internet voting activists convinced the Department of Defense there was too much risk. Paul Lux is an advocate for finding a better way for the County's significant military population to vote. He and nearly half of his 16 person staff are military veterans. They were disappointed progress had been curtailed. Lux said, "It is very unfortunate military voters must follow the same voting process which was used during the Civil War more than 150 years ago."[215]

Lux said that the primary issue raised by Florida politicians was Internet security. He believed a secure voting solution for military voters could be implemented using the Common Access Card, a "Smart" ID card for active-duty military personnel, Selected Reserve, DoD civilian employees, and eligible contractor personnel. The Card is the same in principle as the Estonian ID card.

The Florida legislature has authorized a task force including 32 counties to study new voting enhancements. Mr. Lux said, "The key in considering Internet voting will be to measure the risk versus the benefits".[216] This is something the anti-Internet voting activists have not considered. Lux agrees there is no point in comparing Internet voting to a perfect system which is unlikely to ever be constructed. The task force is scheduled to report its findings by July 1, 2017.

Michigan (2004)

In 2004, the Michigan Democratic Party conducted a Presidential Primary via the Internet. The Party administered the election and provided each voter with a unique identifier and PIN number. To participate, an individual applied for an absentee ballot or voted in person on Election Day. The absentee ballot application was accessed on the Party website. Several candidate campaigns distributed the absentee ballot application to supporters. The application was completed online or printed and returned to the Party by mail or fax. Upon receipt, Party staff checked the application against the state voter file to confirm the application was returned by a registered Michigan voter. Voters could then vote via the Internet. The Internet voting technology was provided by a spin off company of election.com, which had run the Arizona 2000 Internet voting. The Internet voting system used encryption and firewalls to enhance security. Despite warnings from Verified Voting Advisory Board Member Aviel Rubin who said, "Internet voting is not secure. Period."[217] The Executive Chairman of the Michigan Democratic Party, Mark Brewer, deemed the safeguards as adequate.[218]

Forty-six thousand people voted via the Internet, and turnout was twice the 2000 caucus.[219] Mark Brewer said, "We're pleased not only with the number, but with the security and integrity of the Internet voting system."[220] Michigan was the first state to offer Internet voting over such a long period. Voters had a month to cast their votes. In 2000, Arizona offered Internet voting for just a few days before the primary was held. CBS surveyed Michigan voters who cast their ballots on the Internet. The survey showed 67% chose to vote online for the convenience. Ninety percent said that they voted on computers at home, while the rest voted from work or other location.[221]

Some of the candidates challenged Michigan's plan to offer Internet voting, saying it would put minority and low-income voters at a disadvantage. State Party officials said that it simply offered another choice for voters. Researchers at American University and the University of Massachusetts studied the use of Internet voting as an alternative to other methods of absentee voting. Their findings showed Internet voting is not more biased than other absentee voting methods.[222] They also found younger voters were much more likely to choose to vote online.

District of Columbia (2010)

The District of Columbia Board of Elections and Ethics planned to launch a "Digital Vote by Mail" system during the 2010 General Election for absentee, military and overseas voters. The system was composed of two distinct elements: an online blank ballot distribution system, and a system designed to allow for the return of voted ballots. The ballot return system provided voters with the opportunity to upload voted ballots in PDF format to the Board's servers via the Internet. The Open Source Digital Voting Foundation, a non-profit R&D organization now called the Open Source Election Technology Foundation (OSET), provided the architectural design and the ballot generation, secure upload, and distribution software for the project.

At the urging of OSET, the Elections Board decided to conduct a six day testing period for members of the public to discover any vulnerabilities the Internet voting system might have. The testing was open to all individuals requesting credentials to participate. During the testing period, J. Alex Halderman, Ph.D., a member of the Verified Voting Board of Advisors, and a group of his Ph.D. students from the University of Michigan, attacked the system and were able to easily gain complete access. The team was able to modify ballots and collect usernames and passwords.[223] Due to the test results, the portion of the system designed to return voted ballots via the Internet was not used in the 2010 General Election.

The failed test was not a failure of Internet voting. It was a failure by the IT department to create a secure voting system as provided for in the system design. The technical implementation failure was glaring. A new network router was installed and powered on without changing the default password, which is usually "admin", "password", or just blank. This resulted in making it a trivial exercise for the attackers to break in. Although the attackers did the District of Columbia a service by identifying the vulnerability, the method of reporting the problem is questionable. Rather than quickly and discreetly work with the IT department to fix the problems, the students celebrated the challenge of finding holes in the system by causing the computer of a voting system tester to play the University of Michigan fight song each time the voting system's integrity failed.

West Virginia (2010)

Natalie Tennant, the Secretary of State of West Virginia, has an election attitude. In 2010, West Virginia conducted a pilot program, authorized by the state legislature, to provide deployed military and overseas citizens the ability to use Internet voting to cast their ballots with convenience and security. In 2010, 31 states provided military and overseas voters enhanced methods to vote. The methods included electronic delivery of ballots, online access to ballots, and a variety of electronic ballot return options such as fax, email, and uploading through a web portal. Only

West Virginia provided military and overseas citizens the ability to actually cast their ballot online.

During the 2010 general election, 125 West Virginia military and overseas citizens from eight counties cast their ballots online.[224] Secretary Tennant said,

> The number represented a 162 percent increase over the participation in the 2010 primary. The 76 percent online-vote return rate far exceeds the average 58 percent absentee ballot return rate experienced by counties using standard mail as the ballot transmission method.[225]

The state collaborated with county clerks, representatives of the military and overseas communities, and two Internet vendors, Scytl and Everyone Counts. The vendors provided systems with redundant servers to assure system availability to the voters. Cryptographic algorithms were used to securely link voter data with ballot data. No significant deficiencies or concerns were identified with the West Virginia online voting pilot. Tennant said,

> In short, what West Virginia did worked. It was a small program that helped an admittedly small group of voters cast their ballot more conveniently. There were 125 opportunities for something to go wrong, but to our knowledge, nothing did. There will be those who say Internet voting is far too dangerous, that it is rife with the potential for wrongdoing, that it is easily manipulated. I, and election officials across the country, remain vigilant against assaults on every method of voting, whether it be a paper ballot, optical scan machines, touch-screen voting, Internet voting or voting by mail. [226]

Secretary Tennant showed strong leadership in supporting the Internet voting pilot. She sees it as her duty to continue to improve access to voting, for all voters, and to overcome any barriers to the process. Unfortunately, West Virginia is not a wealthy state, and despite a very successful pilot in 2010, budget restrictions prevented Internet voting from moving into the mainstream for its military and overseas citizens.

Americans Elect (2012)

Peter Ackerman, Managing Director of Rockport Capital, Inc., a Boston based venture capital firm, has been active in significant public causes. He founded the

International Center on Nonviolent Conflict and was the founder and Chairman of Americans Elect. The premise behind Americans Elect is politics aren't working for people. The problem must be fixed by changing the way we elect our leaders.[227] Americans Elect planned to create the first nonpartisan, national online Presidential primary.

Americans Elect was incorporated in 2010, and began recruiting delegates for its 2012 Presidential Primary in July 2011. The plan was to host a national online primary in two phases, ending with a convention in June 2012. LBi, a global marketing and technology agency, was hired to design and build AmericansElect.org which would have been America's first secure online Presidential nominating process. The design included a website which would host a national caucus where all registered voters could participate regardless of political affiliation or in what state the voter lived. The website was designed to handle traffic of up to 15-20 million people, and would allow the voters to draft the candidates, vote on a Platform of Questions, and nominate a candidate. In June of 2012, the site would host the first ever nonpartisan political convention to elect a President.

Americans Elect was open to candidates from any party, as well as independents. The drafting began in February, 2012. After several hours, 360,000 delegates drafted 52 possible candidates including Michael Bloomberg, Warren Buffett, Hillary Clinton, Rahm Emanuel, Jon Huntsman, Ron Paul, Condoleezza Rice, and Buddy Roemer.[228] Presidential candidates would have been required to pick a running mate from a different party to attain a balanced ticket. Americans Elect registered as a political party in 29 states.

The online voting process was outlined in great detail. A certain number of clicks was required to narrow down the field of candidates. Three phases of online voting would lead to a June 2012 final candidate, through an Internet-based convention, a process open to all voters, regardless of party affiliation. The design of the voting process was intended to provide a more open nominating process and better choices during the final election.[229]

The first primary ballot was to take place on May 1, 2012, but was cancelled because no candidate received enough clicks to qualify as a candidate. A second failed attempt was held on May 15. On May 17, Americans Elect announced an official end to the nomination process because no candidate had achieved enough clicks. In the summer of 2012, Americans Elect withdrew its name from most state ballots.[230] The Americans Elect website is still online, but has not been updated since 2012. There are no plans for the 2016 general election.

Americans Elect spent $35 million in the online effort.[231] I believe the intentions were laudable, but the implementation approach of a single nationwide voting system was outsized. There is an analogy with healthcare.gov, which attempted to roll out a complex nationwide healthcare insurance system for 36 states. The system eventually worked after a two month delay and expenditures of more than $2 billion.[232] The election system in America is likewise complex. In my opinion, achieving the goals of Americans Elect will require a multiyear state by state effort.

Canada (2014)

In Canada, the term First Nations refers to the indigenous peoples of the country. More than 20 of Canada's 634 recognized First Nations governments have used Internet voting for elections or referendums in the past several years. Many more are considering doing so.[233] According to the Internet Voting Project, a Canadian non-profit which disseminates academic research addressing Internet voting in Canada, "The reasons for Internet voting adoption include hopes of increased civic engagement, increasing voter turnout, and a means of achieving self-government".[234]

Internet voting also is being embraced among local municipalities. Of the 414 municipalities conducting local elections in Ontario, 97 used Internet voting for their 2014 local elections.[235] Nearly 2.4 million voters, approximately one quarter of the Ontario electorate, had the option of voting online.[236] Canadian municipalities have used Internet voting in more elections than any other country in the world, and the Internet Voting Project expects Internet voting to grow.[237]

Utah Primary (2016)

The Utah Republican Party has been in a dispute with the state government since 2014 over whether the State has the right to decide how Republican nominees are selected.[238] As of May 2016, the suit remains unsettled. The state Republican Party decided to enfranchise the out of state registered Utah voters, a progressive party move. The Republicans decided to conduct the March 2016 primary with Internet voting. They worked with Smartmatic, a London based provider of voting technologies and solutions, to develop an online voting system. Nearly 90% of the 27,490 registered voters who registered to vote online did. Voters included local and overseas Utah citizens. Internet voting was for the Presidential candidates only, not other state and local selections which had to be made by the traditional caucus.

Smartmatic reported, "Voters of all ages, from millennials right through to people in their 80s, chose to cast their vote online. Participation was strongest amongst voters aged 56-65."[239] The availability of easy online registration and remote voting resulted in a very inclusive election. Utah Republicans voted online from over 45 countries.[240]

After making their selections, online voting participants were asked for feedback on their experience. Smartmatic reported 94% of respondents described the online voting experience as good, 97% would consider voting online in future elections, and 82% want to see online voting implemented nationwide.[241]

The Internet voting experience was not without criticism. The Verge, an online news site which covers the intersection of technology, science, art, and culture, reported, "The experience for some voters was one of frustration, as they reported being stopped from making their choice by error messages, pages that wouldn't load, and confusing web design."[242] However, the main issue was registration errors. The process for online voter registration was managed by a third party provider, not the online voting platform itself.

Another report described a fake website at ivotingcenter.gop which was set-up by a University of Michigan student during the Utah primary. The site spoofed the legitimate ivotingcenter.us but lacked any voting functionality.[243] If a voter was able to cast a vote at the fake site, it would be a lost vote. However, the actual loss of votes was probably low. The election officials did a good job of sending out clear instructions on how to reach the voting site, how to tell the real one from a fake one, and to access only the legitimate online voting site from the main Utah Republican homepage.

I believe the Utah Republican Party test of Internet voting was successful. It was not perfect, but it showed the potential of Internet voting. Shortly after the primary, James Evans, Chairman of the Utah Republican Party stated:

> We are proud to have taken a leading role in election modernization. By offering online voting, we expanded the number of options citizens have to participate and made voting as convenient as possible. Technology proved key in engaging citizens and bolstering democracy.[244]

Mark Thomas, Director of Elections for Utah, told me, "The key to the future of Internet voting is getting the people to trust it".[245] Recognizing the challenges but embracing the future, Thomas said, "The Internet voting pilot was a good step forward."[246] As to the future of nationwide Internet voting, the Director said, "We will get there."[247] Smartmatic managers agree. Mike Summers, Program Manager - Internet Voting, said, "Clear communication is the key. When the electorate begins to understand the shortcomings of the paper and mail systems in use compared to the advantages of Internet voting, the voters will embrace the Internet approach."[248]

The Constitution gave the states power to decide how to run their elections. In some states, responsibility is further delegated to the parties. So far in this chapter, we have reviewed a Democratic primary in Arizona and a Republican caucus in Utah. Though there were some problems, I believe both used Internet voting successfully.

Los Angeles County, California

Dean Logan is the Registrar-Recorder/County Clerk responsible for conducting federal, state and most local elections in one of the largest and most complex election jurisdictions in the U.S. With 4.9 million registered voters spread across 4,751 square miles, the County has more voters than 42 of 50 states.[249] Los Angeles County's population of 10.02 million reside within 88 cities and 53 unincorporated communities.[250] They vote in more than 500 school, water and other special district's elections. The Clerk's Office conducts approximately 200 city, school, and special district elections annually. Additionally, under the multilingual provisions of the Federal Voting Rights Act, the County is required to produce ballots in ten languages in addition to English.[251]

In September 2009, the County launched the Voting Systems Assessment Project in response to expanding voting system needs and challenges faced by the County. The election officials believed their current voting system had served the voters with accuracy and integrity, but like many voting jurisdictions, the design of the current systems and the age of the equipment is inadequate.

The County election officials concluded none of the current voting machine companies could meet their needs and decided to develop its own specifications for an ideal voting system. The Clerk's Office three goals were:

1) Give current and future Los Angeles County voters an unprecedented opportunity to participate in the assessment and development process.

2) Increase voter confidence in the electoral process through the participatory structure of the project.
3) Synthesize public input and research to acquire or develop a new voting system for the County.

In July 2016, Los Angeles County announced the completion of the first phase of designing the new voting system.[252] The prototype they unveiled remained a paper ballot system but incorporated a touch-screen ballot-marking device. After voters make their selections on the screen, the system will print out a paper ballot for the voter to review and then feed back into the machine for counting the paper ballots at night in the election headquarters. The next step is to develop and release a Request for Proposal for a completely new voting system. Dean Logan hopes to be able to roll out the new system on a limited basis for early voting in the 2018 election, and to convert completely by 2020.[253]

From the onset of the Voting Project, the possibility of Internet voting was never considered. Among the members of the Project's Technical Advisory Committee are well-known anti-Internet voting activists Pamela Smith, President of Verified Voting, and David Wagner, a UC Berkeley computer scientist.[254] Wagner continues to insist on requiring paper trails for all voting systems.[255]

The City of Los Angeles – A Visionary Approach

The City of Los Angeles is the largest, by area and population, of Los Angeles County's 88 cities with a population of 3.9 million. The City has a separate elections department responsible for conducting their local city elections independent of the County. The City is embracing Internet voting with a pilot project for elections of their Neighborhood Councils under the Department of Neighborhood Empowerment's EmpowerLA.

EmpowerLA is a program to increase civic engagement and citizen-based government in the City of Los Angeles, the second largest City in the U.S. Through a network of 96 Neighborhood Councils, the City promotes public participation in government and works to improve government responsiveness to local concerns. EmpowerLA selected La Jolla, California based Everyone Counts Inc. to modernize voting for its citizens.[256] In early 2016 EmpowerLA announced,

EmpowerLA is excited to announce that in addition to having polling locations on election day, 35 of the 96 Neighborhood Councils in the City of Los Angeles are also piloting Online Voting for their elections, which provides an opportunity for voters to register in advance of the election and vote from a desktop computer, a tablet, or a smartphone. In addition, 12 of the 35 are offering Interactive Voice Response (touch-tone phone) voting for their stakeholders. [257]

The City of Los Angeles Internet voting pilot project is limited to voters in 35 of 96 Neighborhood Councils for the election of board members and officers among the 1,800 elected Neighborhood Council members. The pilot project does not currently extend to selecting members of the Los Angeles City Council nor involve County conducted federal and state elections. Stephen Box is Director of Outreach and Communication and Senior Project Coordinator for the Department of Neighborhood Empowerment. When I asked him in May 2016 how the pilot was going, he said it was approximately half completed, adding,

Someone had to be first. We have learned a lot. For example, we quickly realized Internet voting would be the easy part. The harder part is to get accurate and timely voter registrations from citizens in the neighborhoods. I am cautiously optimistic the pilot will be successful.

If the pilot is successful, the City of Los Angeles may conclude it should consider Internet voting for municipal elections. Indeed, voters who choose the Internet voting option are likely to extol the virtues of ease and convenience and begin to clamor for the opportunity to continue to vote via the Internet in Los Angeles City Council and County conducted elections. The seeds of election attitude are being sown in the Neighborhood Councils of the City of Los Angeles. It remains to be seen how fast those seeds may grow.

Travis County, Texas

Dana DeBeauvoir is Travis County Clerk whose duties include supervising the Elections Division located in Austin, Texas. Like many voting jurisdictions, Travis County was looking for a solution to the aging voting machines in use by their 692,000 registered voters. In June 2015, Ms. DeBeauvoir released a Request for Information (RFI) for the design, development, implementation, maintenance, and continued evolution of a new voting system, called STAR-Vote™. Ms. DeBeauvoir said,

> I am thrilled to release the RFI for STAR-Vote™. It will provide an afford-able election system that is Secure, Transparent, Auditable, and Reliable. I believe that it will redefine the polling place by using current technology that can evolve over time as laws, voter needs, and computer systems change.[258]

The 237 page RFI describes the desire to acquire an idealized, modern system but precludes Internet voting, only mentioning the Internet in reference to connect-ing polling locations to Travis County's Voter Registration System through a Voter Check-In Station. [259] She said, "When people stop me in the supermarket and ask, 'When am I going to be able to vote on my cell phone?', I say 'Pretty soon — in about 20 years.'"[260]

I believe it is clear Ms. DeBeauvoir has been influenced by anti-Internet voting activists. The Travis County website has several prominent links on its homepage to "The Future of Internet Voting". The links go to a page listing six articles by anti-Internet voting activists with no mention of ongoing Internet voting in Estonia, Switzerland, Canada or the recent 2016 Utah Republican primary election. These articles compare Internet voting to a perfect system, not to the error-prone voting systems we use today. If Travis County citizens are asking about Internet Voting now, I suspect they will be demanding it in much less than 20 years. A more bal-anced, inclusive approach in the RFI would have invited respondents to consider specifying a path toward Internet voting within a decade, beginning with pilot projects. The excellent work the County has done with the initial RFI could be adapted to Internet voting later.

Internet Ballot Submission

In addition to registering to vote via the Internet and the pilots described in Arizona and elsewhere, states are making progress in allowing ballots to be sub-mitted electronically. Electronic submission via the Internet is not the same as Internet voting. With Internet voting, the voter visits a website, makes selections on a webpage and clicks to vote. Submitting a ballot electronically can be done in two ways:

1) A blank ballot can be downloaded from a website, printed out, filled out, and faxed to the voting precinct.
2) The ballot can be filled out, scanned into a PDF document, and emailed or uploaded through a web portal.

Submitting voted ballots electronically via fax, email, or web portal, is generally reserved for voters who fall under the Federal Uniformed and Overseas Citizens Absentee Voting Act. Following is a summary from the National Conference of State Legislatures of what states allow use of the Internet for voting. [261]

Five states, Alabama, Alaska, Arizona, Missouri and North Dakota, allow some voters to return ballots using a web portal. There are variations in what is allowed. Most states allow the remote submission for military and overseas citizens, but some have restrictive provisions. Missouri offers electronic ballot return for military voters serving in a hostile zone. Idaho allows remote submission only for citizens directly affected by a national or local emergency declared by the Secretary of State.[262] Alabama allows electronic submission only to military and overseas citizens voters outside of U.S. territorial limits and only as a pilot project for the 2016 Primary Election. North Dakota and Arizona permit any military and overseas citizen voter to use the electronic option. Alaska makes it available for any voters.

- Twenty states plus the District of Columbia allow military and overseas citizens voters to return ballots via email or fax: Colorado, Delaware, Idaho, Indiana, Iowa, Kansas, Maine, Massachusetts, Mississippi, Montana, Nebraska, Nevada, New Jersey, New Mexico, North Carolina, Oregon, South Carolina, Utah, Washington and West Virginia.
- Seven states allow military and overseas citizens to return ballots via fax: California, Florida, Hawaii, Louisiana, Oklahoma, Rhode Island and Texas.
- Eighteen states do not allow electronic transmission. Voters must return voted ballots via postal mail: Arkansas, Connecticut, Georgia, Illinois, Kentucky, Maryland, Michigan, Minnesota, New Hampshire, New York, Ohio, Pennsylvania, South Dakota, Tennessee, Vermont, Virginia, Wisconsin, and Wyoming.

Electronic submission is better than all paper processes, but does not match the vision of an election attitude. Neither does the election industry.

The Election Industry

The election industry provides products and services for governmental and non-governmental voting. The companies which build and sell voting hardware, software, and services are private companies which do not reveal their financials. Some large public companies such as Accenture, IBM, and others provide IT related services to election customers, but they do not break out the associated revenue. As a result of these factors, it is difficult to estimate the size of the market. Lori Steele, Founder & Chief Executive Officer at Everyone Counts, Inc., believes the worldwide voting industry market size is approximately $30 billion.[263] She estimates the split between governmental and non-governmental voting industry revenue is roughly 50/50.[264]

The focus of *Election Attitude* is making voting in America convenient and easy for all registered voters. Other than the few trials previously discussed, the voting process does not use the Internet. However, Internet voting is widespread for non-governmental purposes. For example, Eden Prairie, Minnesota based Survey & Ballot Systems offers a cloud based election solution for various types of member organizations such as associations, cooperatives, credit unions, clubs, student governments, unions, and chambers of commerce.

Simply Voting Inc., located in Montreal, Canada, offers similar Internet voting services as the Survey & Ballot System. It also offers an automated system for municipal voting. The company boasts web-based online voting systems serving more than 1,000 organizations in 48 countries. The company claims to organize flawless elections for local governments. However, their municipal customers are mostly small towns. None are in the United States, but they have provided Internet voting services for political party conventions in the U.S. The company does not have clearance from the parties to mention they are customers.[265]

Edmonton, Alberta based eventIQ is a company with an Internet voting service called electionbuddy. The company's target market includes associations, student groups, high schools, and universities. It claims Harvard University, Yale University, University of Kentucky, and University of Maryland among its customers. As of May 2016, the company had conducted 15,391 elections with 2,752,689 votes cast.[266] The following sections will describe companies and organizations focused on technology solutions for governmental voting.

Everyone Counts, Inc.

Lori Steele Contorer, Founder and Chief Executive Officer of La Jolla, California based Everyone Counts, Inc. is an expert in election modernization. She has pioneered cloud based technology to make elections more accessible, affordable, transparent, and secure. Everyone Counts has led successful election administration and voting projects in the United States, Canada, the United Kingdom, Bosnia, Herzegovina, Australia, and more than 100 other countries. The company also provided a transition from vote by mail to secure online voting for the Oscar and Emmy awards.

Ms. Steele Contorer is optimistic about Internet voting. She sees it as the most secure solution to replace the aging machines of today. She believes more than 50% of public voting will be via the Internet by 2024.[267] Part of her optimism comes from the company's eLect® Quad Audit™ Voting and Tabulation System. The System is designed to provide transparency and auditability. For each ballot cast, the System generates four separate audit trails: encrypted machine readable ballot data, an encrypted digital ballot, an encrypted ballot image, and a voter verified paper ballot. Each of the four voting records can be tabulated independently to verify election results. Rather than take a sample, as is often the auditing approach, the System allows election officials to audit 100 percent of the votes.

Other election experts I interviewed believe the only way to verify the software of a voting system is for it to be open source. Although the eLect® Quad Audit™ System uses proprietary software, the company offers an Open Code Advantage™ program which allows an independent third party to review the software under a confidentiality agreement and confirm it is secure and operates as advertised.

Everyone Counts Inc. has a broad portfolio of experience in the U.S. and the world. They have significant Internet experience. When combined with the cloud technologies they have developed, they are positioned to be a major player in public elections. They may gain significant recognition if the EmpowerLA Internet voting project in the City of Los Angeles is successful. Investors will see the potential. In September 2015, Falcon Investment Advisors LLC and Draper Associates invested $20 million in the company. This new round of funding enabled the company to build out its sales and marketing operations as well as accelerate federal certification of its eLect® Quad Audit voting system.

Helios Voting System

Ben Adida created and maintains the Helios Voting System which offers end to end verifiable Internet voting. Dr. Adida holds a Ph.D. in Computer Science from the Cryptography and Information Security Group at MIT. More than 100,000 votes have been cast online using Helios. Dr. Adida describes the Helios approach to voting with three simple attributes:

1)   Private: no one knows how you voted
2)   Verifiable: each voter gets a tracking number
3)   Proven: Helios is open source, vetted by top tier experts, and in use by major organizations[268]

Dr. Adida believes Helios is superior to others because it is verifiable. "True verifiability" means voters are able to confirm the tallying process was performed correctly, not just the recording of their ballot. This is accomplished using a smart ballot tracker. After voters have made their selections on a Helios webpage, their vote is encrypted and sent to the Helios Internet voting server. The Helios web page contains software instructions which make an electronic fingerprint of the encrypted vote, the smart ballot tracker. The tracker ID is similar to the tracking number on a shipping package, except the smart tracking number is based on the actual contents. The voter can visit the Helios Ballot Tracking Center website for the election, enter the smart tracking number and receive confirmation their ballot was received and tallied correctly.

Helios has numerous privacy protections. No one, including the administrators of the Helios Voting system, can examine or alter votes. Since the entire voting system was created with open source software, any independent third party can examine the software instructions and confirm it is accurate. Votes are stored in the Helios database in encrypted form. Helios uses the most advanced cryptographic techniques available to combine the encrypted votes into an encrypted total. Only the voting totals can be decrypted. A Helios election administrator can designate multiple trustees for an election. For example, an administrator could name a trustee from each political party and a completely independent trustee.

In order to decrypt the vote totals, all the trustees must be part of the decryption process.

The Helios Voting System software has been used by the International Association for Cryptologic Research, the Princeton student body, a number of major U.S. universities for faculty appointments and tenure votes, Doctors without Borders, the Association for Computing Machinery, the Technion Israel Institute of Technology, and a number of other non-profit organizations.

Dr. Adida is considering offering Helios for a public election trial in some state, county, precinct, or for overseas voters. However, he is not advocating the use of Helios for public office elections. Dr. Adida said, "We just don't trust that people's home computers are secure enough to withstand significant attacks."[269] He sees a possibility of using Helios for in person precinct voting, but the priority for now remains with online voting in the non-public sector.

There are other systems, such as Scantegrity, Pret-a-Voter, STARVote, and Wombat Voting, which provide true verifiability. They are all paper based voting systems. Continued success by Helios in the non-public sector may inspire politicians or election officials to request pilots for public elections.

Smartmatic

The London based Smartmatic voting service company described the opportunity it sees for voting,

> The free world is moving toward a more participatory model of democracy, where in addition to periodic elections, there will and should be a more continuous flow of opinions between citizens and governments.[270]

Smartmatic provides a wide range of voting services including voter administration, polling location management, voter administration, campaign monitoring, ballot production, training, project management, and auditing. The company operates around the world and claims it has helped hundreds of millions of voters cast over 2.5 billion ballots in government elections. In May 2016, Smartmatic helped automate elections in the Philippines. They printed 56 million ballots and deployed 92,509 vote counting machines in 36,805 polling centers.

In 2014, Smartmatic decided to enter the online voting market. They created a joint venture with Cybernetica, the company which helped Estonia build their I-voting system. The company has been focused on developing a next generation Internet voting system built to accommodate a wide range of customer requirements for election management bodies around the world. On March 22, 2016, Smartmatic provided Internet voting technology for the Utah Republican Party Presidential Caucus.

A conference called "Democracy Rebooted: The Future of Technology in Elections", sponsored by the Atlantic Council, was held in March 2016. Antonio Mugica, CEO of Smartmatic, made some comments about Internet voting. He pointed out that election servers typically are only live and subject to hacking attempts for 8 to 24 hours, during an election. He said that when you have a relatively short window of time, it is extremely easy to protect. He said Internet voting servers, "Can be near perfect".[271]

Scytl

Scytl is a venture capital backed Barcelona, Spain provider of secure electronic voting, election management and election modernization solutions. The company claims to have more than 87% market share in Internet voting worldwide.[272] The challenge in evaluating the creditability of market share claims revolves around the definition of the market. It is much too early to precisely define the Internet voting market. I define Internet voting as casting a ballot in a governmental election online with a computer, smartphone, or tablet. Another way to define Internet voting is by including voting which uses the Internet for any aspect of the election process. For example, Scytl was selected by the Federal Voting Assistance Program of the U.S. Department of Defense to provide a secure online ballot delivery system for overseas military and civilian voters for the 2010 election cycle. Scytl was awarded 9 of the 20 state contracts for states that agreed to participate in the program. The states included New York, Washington, Missouri, Nebraska, Kansas, New Mexico, South Carolina, Mississippi, and Indiana.

Scytl calls its Internet voting solution Remote Voting. Remote Voting includes online voting, phone voting, and electronic ballot delivery. The company has nine states as Remote Voting customers, but most of them did not use actual Internet voting. One exception was Okaloosa County, Florida, which used Internet voting for overseas voters. The results of the project were satisfactory since turnout reached 15%, three times higher than the average for absentee voters. More importantly, 100% of the votes were counted compared to an average 30% of the postal votes. The other states used the Internet for a variety of tasks such as training, election results reporting, and ballot delivery. New York used Scytl to allow military or overseas voters to download their ballot electronically, vote, and send the printed ballot back to New York State by postal mail.

TrustTheVote™ Project

The TrustTheVote Project is sponsored by the Open Source Election Technology ("OSET") Foundation, a nine-year-old non-profit 501.c.3 election technology research institute. Their project team, mostly former Apple, Mozilla, or Netscape employees, call themselves social entrepreneurs. They are not a think tank or lobbying group. While they urge caution about Internet voting and do not believe it is feasible in the short term, they are working to build an election technology framework which election officials can adapt and deploy.

The TrustTheVote Project Election Technology Framework ("ElectOS™") is designed to facilitate all aspects of the voting process including registration, voting, and reporting of results. Technology for election officials will enable them to manage elections, register voters, and count ballots. Each of the technology areas within the framework includes one or more applications. The applications are free and can be tailored and deployed by local governments.

Unlike today's proprietary voting machines, these applications run on non-proprietary off the shelf hardware. The TrustTheVote Project will provide a list of hardware, which meets TrustTheVote Project specifications. Systems integration services are required to meet local regulatory and user experience requirements of each jurisdiction and adapt the open source software to local regulatory requirements where necessary. Current voting machine companies and other qualified companies will be able to provide the systems integration and on-going support of the technology. In my opinion, it is unlikely the current voting systems companies will participate.

The TrustTheVote Project software was deployed in part in May 2016. Virginia is using the Voter Services Portal component of the framework. Sixteen states will participate in an upcoming testing of the VoteStream component for elections reporting. The framework applications use a combination of mobile devices, local servers, and the Internet for parts of the election administration process. It is not used for casting votes. That part is planned for the future.

In an interview with Gregory Miller, Chair of the Open Source Election Technology Foundation, he explained the Project's vision as having three phases.

- Phase 1 – Election administration apps for online voter registration, election results reporting, poll books, ballot design, generation, and distribution, and election management services.
- Phase 2 – A complete voting system for cast and counting ballots using tablets, printers, and OpScanners with a paper ballot of record.
- Phase 3 – Complete certification of the voting system and a robust repository service for distribution of the open source software and a finished Framework that can support future types of balloting including remote online casting once that is possible, certified, and legal to deploy.

When questioned when Phase 3 will be developed, Miller said, "At least two Presidential election cycles, perhaps three." The pessimism may in part stem from the Foundation's experience with TrustTheVote software used by Washington, D.C. in 2010. Mr. Miller and his team have developed a deep understanding of the entire election system process from the user application, through the network, to the backend applications and databases. They believe, and I agree, the user application is the easier part. To have a verifiable, accurate, secure, and reliable voting system requires significant planning at all levels—from the so-called "edge" where ballot casting can take place (e.g., a smartphone or personal digital device) to the "core" (e.g., the data center), where most of the challenges and vulnerabilities to be addressed exist—not just in technology, but process and policy as well.

Miller's ten-year timeframe seems long, but I agree the changes needed to today's approach are significant. The challenges are complicated, but in my opinion, solvable.

Blockchain

In November 2008, a paper was posted on the Internet by Satoshi Nakamoto, "Bitcoin: A Peer-to-Peer Electronic Cash System".[273] The paper described a system where Bitcoin, a digital currency, can be used to buy and sell goods and services or to just buy and hold the Bitcoin. Currencies such as the U.S. dollar, the Canadian dollar, or the German Deutschmark are called fiat currencies. Fiat money is currency a government has declared to be legal tender for buying and selling. Some people buy foreign currency and hold on to it as an investment, just like stocks, bonds, or commodities.

To buy or sell Bitcoin requires having a digital wallet. I acquired mine in 2013 from Coinbase, a San Francisco startup with more than $100 million of venture capital behind it. As of the end of 2015, there were almost 13 million digital wallets and more than 100,000 merchants who accepted Bitcoin in payment for goods and services.[274] The most popular merchant is WordPress.com, a website which offers free hosting of blogs, but offers various enhancements for purchase.

My first Bitcoin purchase was for a shirt from Overstock.com. At checkout, I was presented with the normal dialog. "How would you like to pay for your purchase?" The choices were credit card, Overstock Store Card, PayPal, and Bitcoin. I selected Bitcoin. A dialog box then appeared with a QR code, such as you see in magazines, on promotional mailings, and on TSA posters in the waiting line at airports. Then I opened my Coinbase digital wallet on my iPhone and scanned the QR code. The transaction was completed. Use of Bitcoin is in the early stage but, by the end of 2015, there were more than 100,000 Bitcoin transactions per day worldwide.

In the U.S., having a digital wallet and buying things with Bitcoin is not really necessary. Most Americans have easy access to a credit cards for that purpose. However, in some countries, large numbers of people do not have credit cards or don't trust their government's oversight on currency. Brazil and the Philippines currently have the most digital wallets and transactions.[275]

Bitcoin is not the only digital currency, although it is the most popular. Alternative digital currencies to Bitcoin are called Altcoins. The leading Altcoins are Ripple, Litecoin, Ethereum, Dash, Dogecoin, Peercoin, Stellar, MaidSafeCoin, and Bitshare. The common ingredient in all digital currencies is blockchain technology. A blockchain provides the underlying technology infrastructure which enables the digital currencies to be secure, private, and not subject to fraud.

A blockchain is a distributed ledger. It is a place where each transaction is recorded, except the exact copies of the ledger are recorded and stored on servers operated by people who are part of the digital currency network. There can be thousands of servers. The more copies of the ledger, the better. The reason for multiple copies is that blockchain technology requires consensus. All of the server copies of the ledger have to be in agreement. If someone hacks into one of the servers and tampers with the ledger, the attempt will be rejected because the majority of the servers will not agree. The requirement for consensus in the blockchain creates a very secure system.

A blockchain is not limited to handling digital currencies. Just as a Bitcoin transaction can be recorded on a blockchain, contracts and assets can also be recorded. Transactions associated with the contract or asset are stored in a block and blocks are then linked to each other, hence the name blockchain. A block is updated by consensus of all the servers who are running the blockchain software. The consensus is based on rules agreed upon by parties to the transaction. Once the record of a transaction is placed in the blockchain, it can never be altered. Records of transactions are stored at multiple locations which all compare their blockchain to all the others. As a result, discrepancies are instantly identifiable. Systems built on a blockchain include rules specifying what each user can see or do, depending on their role. The result is that each transaction can be trusted because it is secure, private, authenticated, and verifiable. Nearly every industry and type of transaction can potentially benefit from blockchain technology.

Don Tapscott, author of *Blockchain Revolution: How the Technology Behind Bitcoin is Changing Money, Business and the World*, sees voting as a natural choice to take advantage of blockchain technology. He said,

> Blockchain is a global database – an incorruptible digital ledger of economic transactions which can be programmed to record not just financial transactions, but virtually everything of value and importance to humankind. Examples are birth and death certificates, marriage licenses, deeds and titles of ownership, educational degrees, financial accounts, records of medical procedures, insurance claims, votes, transactions between smart objects, and anything else that can be expressed in code. A blockchain ledger is accurate because mass collaboration constantly reconciles it.[276]

Peter Williams, Chief Technology Officer for Big Green Innovations at IBM Corporation, described how blockchain technology might be used to track car ownership and registration.

> I recently bought a used car, for which the previous owner had lost the title document. The ensuing paper chase and time wasted dealing with my local DMV prompted my usual frustrated thought that "there has to be a better way!" With a blockchain, there is a better way. Imagine my

car – model, VIN number, registration number - as an entry in my state's car ownership "ledger". All the parties to its lifecycle – owners, DMV, financier, insurer, police – would have access to the entry to record or view transactions such as change of ownership, registration, loan-pay-off and so on. Transferring ownership would no longer be a paper chase – the previous owner would record online that she had sold the car to me, and I would record that I had bought the car from her. Authenticity could be confirmed by including some details from our respective driving licenses, say. The paired records would be taken as proof of sale, and transfer of title would be instant. DMV would "see" the transaction from its own replicated copy, and automatically issue a new title and registration certificate – which need exist only electronically. Transfer of financial obligations would also be automatic. The whole lifecycle would be encrypted and secure. The previous owner would be able to see her portion of the car's history, and I would see mine.

Many of us have been involved in automotive transactions, but may not have thought of the details as a single process. Mr. Williams describes the process in more detail,

Now go further – each owner could have their mechanics enter maintenance and emissions check data so that they could prove the service history; if they have an insurance transponder, they could even release summary data to buyers showing how the car had been driven. If certain parts and panels were encoded I could confirm that those codes remained original (meaning that the car had not been in an accident); and so on. Overall, the benefits to me in terms of speed and reduced hassle would be huge; to law and order, likewise; and in terms of reduced costs from processing paperwork, sorting out mismatches and so on, also huge![277]

Like Mr. Williams, I believe innovators will bring blockchain technology into all aspects of business and consumer life just like the Internet did. The Internet was initially only used for file sharing and messaging, but it continuously evolved and became more useful. That is what I see happening with blockchain technology. So does Melanie Swan, author of *Blockchain: Blueprint for a New Economy*. She said,

Not only is there the possibility that blockchain technology could reinvent every category of monetary markets, payments, financial services, and economics, but it might also offer similar reconfiguration possibilities to all industries, and even more broadly, to nearly all areas of human endeavor.[278]

On May 16, 2016, Jerry Cuomo, IBM's Vice President for Blockchain, testified before the President's Commission on Enhancing National Cyber Security. Cuomo said that he believes this technology could dramatically change the way financial systems are secured and that government, technology companies and industries should work together to advance blockchain to enhance national security. IBM has some creditability in this area. Eighty years ago, IBM helped the U.S. government create the Social Security system. This was a bold initiative at the time. Cuomo said, "It was the most complex financial system ever developed".[279] Currently, IBM is taking a proactive approach to work with the government to advance blockchain technology. The goal is to make financial systems of the future more efficient and secure. Cuomo said,

Blockchain has inherent qualities that provide trust and security, but to fulfill its promise, the core technology must be further developed using an open-source governance model to make it deployable on a grand scale. Government agencies can become early adopters of blockchain applications. In addition, government has a key role to play in certifying the identities of participants in blockchain-based systems. Blockchain has tremendous potential to help transform business and society, but it's so strikingly different from what people are used to that many business and government leaders are adopting a wait-and-see attitude. We applaud judicious caution, but, at the same time, we believe that organizations and institutions that don't quickly assess the potential of blockchain and begin experimenting with it risk falling behind as the world undergoes what we see as a tectonic shift.[280]

Blockchain is potentially a game-changer in other than financial areas. For example, using the blockchain for Internet voting may provide significant advantages to the current, proprietary electronic voting systems. One of the key features of blockchain technology is it uses free, open-source, peer-reviewed software. Open source software is easily viewed by anyone. It is the opposite of proprietary software which is tightly controlled by vendors. Transparency is particularly important for the software used for voting, and is generally embraced by progressive voting enthusiasts. Much of the software behind today's voting systems is proprietary. No one except the proprietary owners can say for certain exactly what the programming instructions in the software do. With open source software, anyone can inspect the software and see exactly how it works and what it does. Independent auditors can review the software instructions and certify the software for voting officials.

Open source software is developed by a community of developers. Although there is no central management structure, open source software evolves rapidly because almost anyone can contribute to it. This might include a large software project contributed by IBM or Google. It also could be software to enable a new gadget that a student in Eastern Europe contributed. A system administrator at XYZ Company may be looking for a certain kind of software and makes the need known on the Internet. Meanwhile, someone in another part of the world may have just written such software, and be happy to give it away to anyone who needs it. In theory, perhaps such global collaboration shouldn't work so well, but it does. Developers like the fact if they find a bug in open source software they can either fix it or report it to others in the community. They know the software is open for all to see, errors will be fixed, and the results can be inspected. There is a dedicated community supporting open source software.

A myth about open source software is it is popular because it is free. In the case of open source Linux software, free versions are available. This makes it easy for students to learn. Although most open source software is free, numerous companies, large and small, provide consulting, installation, and support services for a fee.

Blockchain technology for voting offers other possible advantages. The software is readily available. Experts agree it is secure. Although there have been breaches and other problems with some Bitcoin related companies, there are no known cases of Bitcoin's blockchain being hacked. When a vote is cast, it is encrypted and stored in the blockchain. The vote will be counted, but the privacy of the voter is protected. Independent auditors can confirm election results. Cost comparisons of handling votes in a new way are not yet available, but Wall Street firms see the potential of significant savings when handling financial transactions on the blockchain instead of in the traditional manner.[281]

The use of blockchain technology reduces the trust level required from the organizers. At first, this may sound more like a disadvantage. A simple example may clarify the point. Suppose an American city has 500 polling places, each with blockchain technology on a server. Each server would contain a database of all votes cast. The same database would be on all of the servers. When a new vote is cast, it is recorded in the local database and shared with all of the other 499 servers. The blockchain technology checks to make sure all the databases are in agreement. If someone tampers with a vote on one of the servers, the change would be detected by the other servers. The tampered vote would be rejected because consensus is required to confirm a transaction. Voters are not just trusting one server, they are trusting the consensus of many servers. Open source blockchain technology has potential to solve the problems of lack of adequate security and integrity of current voting systems. Entrepreneurs are recognizing the potential and are hard at work customizing blockchain technology to meet the specific needs of voting.

IBM's Cuomo has put blockchain in the genes. His son has an election attitude. He is interning at IBM for the summer (2016) and is building a demonstration voting app using Hyperledger blockchain technology. Hyperledger is a global collaboration of major corporations in finance, banking, Internet of Things, supply chain, technology, and manufacturing. The following sections describes what two entrepreneurs are doing with blockchain technology for voting.

Follow My Vote

Adam Ernest has been an entrepreneur since he was ten years old. He earned the nickname "The Candyman" from a business he started by selling candy out of his backpack to fellow schoolmates. In 2004, he graduated from Virginia Tech Pamplin College of Business with a Bachelor of Science degree in Marketing Management. He then followed his entrepreneurial instincts at a number of companies including Enterprise Rent-A-Car, MediaWhiz Holdings LLC, Matomy Media Group, and Wicked Efficiency, Inc. Adam cast his first vote in 2000, at age 18.

When reflecting on the catastrophic errors of the 2000 election, as described by Ted Selker in *Scientific America*,[282] Adam got enthused about the possibility of using blockchain technology to improve the voting process. Adam explained "Elections seem to happen in a black box and nobody knows what is really going on. There has to be a better way."[283] In July 2012, he became Co-Founder & CEO of Follow My Vote. Mr. Ernest's vision is, "To create an open source end to end verifiable elections system on the Internet".[284]

Mr. Ernest and his colleagues established Follow My Vote as a benefit corporation. A benefit corporation is a type of United States for-profit corporate entity, authorized in 30 U.S. states and the District of Columbia. The charter of a benefit corporation includes proof of having a positive impact on society, workers, the community, and the environment. The intent is to be profitable within those guidelines. The benefitcorp.net website describes benefit corporations as follows,

> Benefit corporations are leaders in a global movement to use business as a force for good. Both meet higher standards of accountability and transparency. Both create the opportunity to unlock our full human potential and creativity to use the power of business for the higher purpose of solving society's most challenging problems.[285]

Benefit corporations may have an advantage in attracting new, young talent. Millennials are expected to grow to 75% of the workforce by 2025.[286] A Deloitte Millennial Survey found, 77% believe a company's purpose is part of the reason they chose to work there.[287] A key feature of a benefit corporation is it gives prospective employees confidence a company is legally committed to their mission. Mr. Ernest is targeting millennials as employees and as funders through kickstarter donations.[288] As of May 2016, 71 kickstarter members had signed up to support the Follow My Vote vision. Adam believes the millennials can think outside the box and accomplish things experts have said cannot be done.

Follow My Vote's ambition is to build a secure online voting platform which will allow for greater election transparency. Transparency means independent third parties can see the software and how it operates. Proprietary software being used today is not transparent. Follow My Vote believes past, present, and future voting machines can be extremely vulnerable and have the potential to unfairly influence the outcome of elections. The company sees a lack of transparency in our elections and a lack of security in the election systems. Follow My Vote plans to bring transparency into elections without compromising voter privacy, and to provide a way to mathematically prove election results are accurate. The technology the company is building will allow voters to cast their votes online and follow their votes into the ballot box to ensure their vote was safely and securely stored without being changed or altered in any way. This company also believes blockchain technology can significantly reduce the cost of elections. "This would free up taxpayer money to be spent on important things like improving the quality of education and rebuilding our crumbling infrastructure."[289]

Using a webcam and a government issued ID to confirm identity, voters could remotely and securely log in and vote. The voter would scan and send his or her photo ID to an election official. Then they would show themselves in front of the webcam to confirm his or her identify. The election official then would provide a Voter ID via the website.

After a person selected candidates, they would use their unique Voter ID to virtually open the ballot box, locate their vote, and confirm it is both present and correct. Voters could then watch the election progress in real time as votes are cast. Indecisive voters or voters who may have been coerced to cast a certain vote could return to the system and switch his or her vote at any time before the election deadline closes.

Follow My Vote plans to demonstrate the power and convenience of their technology by offering online voting to the public in what they are calling, "a parallel election alongside the 2016 U.S. Presidential Election". By participating in Follow My Vote's Parallel Presidential Election of 2016,

> You are taking a stand for what you believe in. You are telling your government that you want to have the right to vote conveniently online, in a secure and verifiably honest way, in the next government-sponsored election. A vote in Follow My Vote's Parallel Presidential Election of 2016 is a vote for honesty and transparency when it comes to our elections.[290]

> After all, if you cannot count your vote and see it successfully and safely stored in the ballot box with your own eyes, how can you even be certain that your vote was actually counted?[291]

Blockchain Technologies Corporation

Nick Spanos is Chairman of Blockchain Technologies Corporation headquartered in New York. He attended American Community Schools in Athens, Greece. He then studied computer science at New York Institute of Technology. For the last 30 years, Mr. Spanos has been a serial entrepreneur. His company is a blockchain and cryptocurrency software technology company and startup accelerator. While blockchain technology is very new to most, Mr. Spanos has been involved with this technology since its infancy in 2008. Mr. Spanos' long history in technology is matched by his long history in the world of voting and elections. He has helped plan, audit, and manage elections in many parts of the country including Florida, New York, and Texas.

America's voting machine technology – or lack thereof – is a looming crisis since many states are using antiquated voting machines which are very expensive and difficult to maintain. Mr. Spanos sees blockchain technology as the best direction to improve future voting. The following four blockchain features sum up his belief.

1) Include verifiable blockchain software source code for voting machines
2) Prevent voter fraud by eliminating the possibility of more votes than registered voters
3) Provide instant, transparent and incorruptible voting data
4) Make blockchain software available at a very low cost and easy to implement[292]

Blockchain Apparatus, one of Blockchain Technologies Corporation's companies, has developed a hybrid voting system which includes paper ballots, scanners, and a blockchain. The system uses innovative techniques I have not found in any other voting system. The hardware is off the shelf and non-proprietary. The software is open source. The voter fills out a familiar paper ballot and places it in a scanner at the polling place. The scanner records the vote in a "mini blockchain" in the local voting server. When the poll closes, the votes are recorded in the FlorinCoin blockchain. The totals for all the votes cast are encrypted and stored in the Bitcoin blockchain. The system was used successfully in the Libertarian Party of Texas election in April 2016.[293]

When asked when the blockchain technology will be used for online voting, Mr. Spanos said,

It will take time. People have to be comfortable and confident in the system they use. Candidates will also need time to adopt a new way of thinking. Every election has multiple candidates, each of whom is sure they are going to win. When the election is over, the losers will be quick to challenge the voting system as the reason for their loss. Ultimately, voters and candidates will realize the blockchain will lead to fair and honest elections because the power of the blockchain ledger will ensure all votes are counted correctly and cannot be altered. The result is an honest and fair election.[294]

Blockchain technology is evolving very quickly, perhaps even faster than the Internet developed. A group of banks, including JP Morgan Chase and Citigroup, have successfully tested blockchain on credit-default swaps, financial contracts which allow buyers of debt to eliminate possible losses arising from defaults. The results of these tests indicate blockchain could gain a foothold on Wall Street as a record-keeping system. Credit swaps represent a very large number of outstanding contracts, and the process of matching buyers, sellers, and trades, in the legacy systems currently used by banks, is a challenge. In a March 2016 test by banks, including J.P. Morgan Chase & Co. and Citigroup Inc., $6.7 trillion face value in outstanding contracts, which normally were spread across multiple servers, were replaced with a blockchain network. The test was considered a success[295] The process is a long way from being ready to implement for live trades, but I believe it will happen.

Voting has unique aspects to it, but it also has similarities to financial transactions. Treating votes as transactions can create a blockchain to keep track of the tallies of the votes. As described by Follow My Vote and Blockchain Technologies Corporation, everyone can agree on the final count because they can trust the blockchain technology. Due to the blockchain audit trail, people can verify no votes were changed or removed, and no illegitimate votes were added. Using this technology, everyone can know the reported election results are truly accurate.

Mobile

There are three technology components to having election attitude: the Internet, blockchain technology, and mobile smartphones. Previously, the Internet was on your PC, now the Internet is everywhere we are. The shift to mobile is clear. There are now more global mobile Internet users than desktop users.[296] The world is said to have surpassed the mobile moment when the number of mobile devices equals the number of people on the planet.[297] Mobile retail e-commerce sales, purchases made from smartphones and tablets, in the United States was $57 billion in 2014.[298] It is expected to be nearly double for 2016 and nearly triple in 2019. The mobile Internet can be accessed from a smartphone or a tablet. Some people call the large screen smartphones phablets – larger than a normal smartphone and smaller than a normal tablet. The definition of phone or tablet is blurring, but the point is these devices are mobile. We carry them with us, whether in a pocket, purse, on our wrists, or in a briefcase.

Mobile devices are an ideal platform for voting. Use of a mobile device can be private. If someone tries to coerce you to vote a certain way, you can go somewhere private to vote by yourself. Hopefully, most voting systems will be designed to allow multiple votes, and your last vote is the one which counts. As mentioned previously, having multiple opportunities to vote up until the polls close reduces the possibility of coercion.

Mobile devices also have the advantage of superior security. Even though there have been reports of malicious software infecting mobile devices and gaining unauthorized access to pictures, contacts, or text messages, the ability of malware gaining access to the inside of another app on a mobile device is less likely. Dr. Ben Adida at Helios Voting Systems sees mobile as a possible means to reduce the risk of a home PC malware ecosystem.[299]

Another proponent of mobile devise voting, Jason Soroko, Manager of Security Technologies at Entrust, an IT security company, said,

> The security that you get out of the box from a mobile operating system already exceeds what you can buy with traditional desktop PC endpoint security. In a world where most of us mix our usage of PCs, smartphones and tablets, it's a great opportunity to take advantage of the strength of the computers we carry in our pockets.[300]

In a research article, "Experimentation Using Short-Term Spectral Features for Secure Mobile Internet Voting Authentication", published in 2015, three researchers at Durban University of Technology in Durban, South Africa have developed an experimental system for secure Internet voting using mobile devices. The goal of the research was achieving the following eight characteristics:

1) Accuracy - Impossible for a valid vote to be excluded, altered or to include an invalid vote in the final counting.
2) Privacy - Inability to link a voter to the vote he or she cast; i.e., anonymity.
3) Verifiability - System adjudged verifiable if a voter, an observer, or anyone can autonomously verify all the cast votes were correctly tallied.
4) Eligibility - Invulnerability such that system permits only eligible voters to vote, vote only once, and nobody can vote more than once or vote on behalf of others.

5) Convenience - Enable voters to vote easily and quickly and with minimal equipment and with no special expertise.

6) Mobility - No geographical restriction with respect to where voters decide to cast their vote. This requirement also implies the system is available and accessible during the voting phase regardless of where the voter decides to cast his or her vote.

7) Flexibility - System allows diversity of ballot question formats including open-ended questions.

8) Incoercible - System is coercion resistant and prevents efforts to manipulate the manner in which a vote is cast, influences a voter to abstain, or represent a valid voter by obtaining the voter's credentials.[301]

To meet these goals, the researchers proposed a Secure Mobile Internet Voting architecture using a voice biometric based authentication module. The technology allows for the confirmation of the identity of a person based on their voice. This is similar to Apple's iPhone TouchID feature which provides identity verification based on a biometric fingerprint. The advantage of a voice biometric is it can work on any mobile device, not just Apple.

The voting solution described by the South African researchers could provide a paradigm shift for the implementation of Internet voting. The experiments leveraged the Internet, mobile devices, GPS location services, Near Field Communication technology, like Apple Pay, and voice biometric authentication. The secure mobile Internet voting architecture the Durban researchers developed fulfilled all eight of the security requirements. At this time, the architecture is in the research stage. Combined with blockchain technology, the South African research may prove to hold a key ingredient for secure voting in the future.

Despite impressive progress in trials, innovation by new companies, and promising research, there remain considerable challenges to Internet voting. The most frequently mentioned concerns are related to security. This important topic is addressed in the next chapter.

CHAPTER 5

Cybersecurity

In chapter 2, I described the impending crisis with old, unreliable, and insecure voting machines. In chapter 3, I discussed the numerous ways in which we trust the Internet with health records, monetary transactions, and many other aspects of our lives. In chapter 4, I described innovation by researchers and startup companies who see Internet voting as an opportunity to improve democracy by increasing voter participation. Despite these developments, many computer science experts believe security is inadequate for Internet voting. They also believe consumers and election staff are not sufficiently aware of the security risks of Internet voting.

In this chapter, I will discuss the key Internet security issues. I will use the term cybersecurity as an umbrella term referring to computer security and IT security. Cybersecurity concerns the protection of information systems from theft or damage to the hardware, software, and information stored on the systems. Cybersecurity also refers to protection against disruption or interference with the services systems provide.

The Internet

In order to understand the Internet security issue, it is necessary to understand how the Internet works. All information which travels across the Internet is split into packets. Every email, webpage, instant message, tweet, FaceTime video chat, or Internet Protocol telephone call is broken up into packets which then traverse the Internet. An average packet contains between five and ten thousand zeroes and ones, or bits. The structure of these packets is made up of headers and payload. The headers contain information such as the packet's source and destination address while the payload contains the actual data being transmitted. The packets move across the Internet by traveling between specialized computers called routers. The packets may not all take the same route from source to destination, but they all end up at the same destination. The routers look at each packet and determine where it should go next. Typically, a packet may take ten to fifteen hops from one router to another before it gets to its destination. Then, the packets get reassembled into an email, webpage, instant message, tweet, FaceTime video chat, or telephone call.

Security in all these transactions is critical and needs to be taken seriously because the Internet itself is completely insecure. It is similar to a 1950's party telephone line where multiple parties were actually sharing the same network. Since only one person could make a call at a time, you might pick up a party phone line and find out your neighbor was already using it. Then, if you could overcome the temptation to listen in, you had to wait your turn to use it. The Internet also is a shared network. As our emails, webpages, and IP telephone calls travel from origin to their destination, a clever snooper could use various tools to inspect or "sniff" the packets to see the contents of the payload. If they are very inventive, they could potentially make changes to the data in the packets and then assemble them back into the email, webpage, or IP telephone call. Fortunately, there are many tools and techniques which can be applied to the Internet to make it secure enough for our many uses, and stop interception.

The key to making the Internet more secure is encryption technology, one of the most powerful technologies ever devised. The most basic approach to using encryption is to use ciphers to scramble messages. The concept of encryption has been around for thousands of years. One of the simplest examples of a substitution cipher is the Caesar cipher, which is said to have been used by Julius Caesar to communicate with his army.[302] Caesar used a very basic cipher technique of shifting each letter in a message. The unencrypted message, called plaintext, uses the alphabet. The encrypted version of the message, called ciphertext, is the alphabet shifted 19 characters to the right. An A would be replaced with a T, a B with a U, etc.

```
Plaintext:   A B C D E F G H I J K L M N O P Q R S T U V W X Y Z

Ciphertext:  T U V W X Y Z A B C D E F G H I J K L M N O P Q R S
```

Figure 2. Ciphertext alphabet with a shift of 19

Caesar informed his generals in person of the shift so they could decipher his messages. Even if the enemy intercepted one of Caesar's messages, it would be useless, since only Caesar's generals could read it.

An example of a message with a 19 character shift is THE FAULT, DEAR BRUTUS, LIES NOT IN OUR STARS BUT IN OURSELVES. The message would be enciphered as MAX YTNEM, WXTK UKNMNL, EBXL GHM BG HNK LMTKL UNM BG HNKLXEOXL.[303]

Ciphers are used today although they are exponentially more sophisticated than what the Romans used. Using complex mathematics, the contents of payloads can be scrambled, or encrypted, in such a way only the intended recipient is able to unscramble, or decrypt, the information being sent. Millions of people recognize this technique enables them to put their credit card number into a secure web transaction in a way only the server at the other end is able to read it. People are realizing their credit card number may be safer on the Internet than it is if they provide it to a stranger over a toll free number for a catalog purchase or to a waiter in a restaurant.

A technology called SSL (Secure Sockets Layer) is a protocol which has been securing web transactions using modern day ciphers for more than 20 years. More recently it has been superseded by the much more secure TLS (Transport Layer Security) protocol though the umbrella term for encrypted communications technology is still referred to as SSL. The concept is to make communications between your web browser and a web server secure so a hacker or snooper somewhere in between cannot read what you send the server or what the server sends to you.

Let's consider the use of SSL in an Internet voting context. When you are ready to vote, you would visit an election server run by a state, county, or a vendor on their behalf. For example, you might visit https://election.state.us. The s in https:// is generally used to signify the server is using the SSL security technology. SSL uses encryption keys to scramble information. The keys are in pairs, referred to as a public key and a private key, which are different but mathematically related. Anyone can use a server's public key, but the private key is stored securely on the server. The encryption is performed using the keys and a combination of complex mathematical protocols called cipher suites.

After the election server receives the request from the voter's browser, the server sends the browser a digital security certificate containing the server's public key. The browser inspects the certificate to ensure it is legitimate. The browser then uses the server's public key to digitally sign any data requested by the server such as a voter registration PIN. Only the webserver can use its private key to decrypt the information sent by the browser. The webserver and the browser are then able to send information back and forth in a secure manner. For example, the election server would send the appropriate ballot to the voter's browser, and the voter would make his or her selections and send the completed ballot back to the server.

Encryption is a powerful ingredient for secure Internet voting. Vint Cerf, recognized as one of the 'fathers of the Internet', and I are Fellows of the Institute of Electrical and Electronic Engineers. We served together on the board of the Global Internet Project, a public policy group which helped global political leaders and staffs understand the capabilities of the Internet in the mid 1990s, and resist the temptation to regulate it. I know of no one who knows more about the capabilities and limitations of the Internet. He told me his perspective on Internet voting,

> The Internet has evolved from its earliest operational incarnation in 1983. In the interim three decades, new transmission and security technologies have been developed and incorporated into the system. Smart phones have appeared. I think it is feasible to develop safe, secure and verifiable online voting. The goal need not be perfection, but something much better than our present olio of systems that have many demonstrated flaws. Cryptography for confidentiality and for strong authentication is a key ingredient for any online voting system. Hardware-reinforced cryptography is not only feasible but also a cost-effective way of backstopping software security systems. Such facilities can be used for all transactions, not only voting, and thus the cost can be spread over a wide range of applications.

Properly installed, high quality encryption software can prevent intruders from gaining access to information they are not authorized to have. At some point in the future, there may be a combination of people, networked computers, and schemes which would enable information encrypted with today's technology to be decoded. However, by then, the strength of the encryption technology also will have advanced. Using encryption enables people to perform secure transactions using an insecure network. Bruce Schneier, renowned security technologist and Chief Technology Officer of Resilient Systems, Inc. said,

Trust the math. Encryption is your friend. Use it well, and do your best to ensure that nothing can compromise it. That's how you can remain secure even in the face of the NSA [National Security Agency].[304]

Even if a message or a vote is encrypted and transmitted accurately to the intended recipient, it is necessary for security to know who sent the encrypted message. The general term for confirming the identity of the sender is called authentication.

Authentication

There was a cartoon by Peter Steiner in the July 5, 1993, issue of *The New Yorker* showing a dog at a PC speaking to another dog watching from the floor. The caption was, "On the Internet nobody knows you're a dog."[305] With voting, it is extremely important to know the identity of the dog. A login and password is not sufficient for Internet voting. In Estonia, every citizen has a government issued chip card representing their individual ID. They use it to pay taxes, retrieve health records, and to vote. In the United States, there has been considerable debate about national ID cards. Some feel it would lead to government surveillance and a national database subject to hackers. Others see national ID cards as essential to protect our borders.

There are numerous ways to provide authentic identification. One alternative is to use passports or driver licenses. Passports issued since 2007 contain chips which can work with biometric facial recognition technology. Biometrics is the measurement and statistical analysis of people's physical or behavioral characteristics used to verify their identity. For example, the South African researchers described in chapter 4 developed an authentication technique using biometric voices. Another approach to authenticating identification is using biometric fingerprints like Apple's iPhone TouchID. An iPhone user can train the TouchID software to recognize up to ten fingers. Once trained, the iPhone can recognize you with a simple touch of a finger. Apple explains the security of TouchID as follows,

Every fingerprint is unique, so it is rare that even a small section of two separate fingerprints are alike enough to register as a match for Touch ID. The probability of this happening is 1 in 50,000 for one enrolled finger.

This is much better than the 1 in 10,000 odds of guessing a typical 4-digit passcode. Although some passcodes, like "1234", may be more easily guessed, there is no such thing as an easily guessable fingerprint pattern. Instead, the 1 in 50,000 probability means it requires trying up to 50,000 different fingerprints until potentially finding a random match. But Touch ID only allows five unsuccessful fingerprint match attempts before you must enter your passcode, and you can't proceed until providing it.

Touch ID doesn't store any images of your fingerprint. It stores only a mathematical representation of your fingerprint. It isn't possible for someone to reverse engineer your actual fingerprint image from this mathematical representation. The chip in your device also includes an advanced security architecture called the Secure Enclave which was developed to protect passcode and fingerprint data. Fingerprint data is encrypted and protected with a key available only to the Secure Enclave. Fingerprint data is used only by the Secure Enclave to verify that your fingerprint matches the enrolled fingerprint data. The Secure Enclave is walled off from the rest of the chip and the rest of iOS. Therefore, iOS and other apps never access your fingerprint data, it's never stored on Apple servers, and it's never backed up to iCloud or anywhere else. Only Touch ID uses it, and it can't be used to match against other fingerprint databases.[306]

The key element to guarantee secure Internet voting is to establish you are who you say you are. A centralized national database is not required. One example of an alternative to a national database is to physically go to the voter registration office and present your credentials. Once your credentials confirm you are who you say you are, the voter office issues a code. The voter can use a voting app to scan the code into his or her iPhone. The app requires TouchID. From then on, you can vote on the Internet using the app. It will only work for you because it requires your fingerprint. When the vote arrives at the Internet voting server, the server will know it was you who cast the vote. If someone coerces you, you can go outside and vote again. Your last vote will be the one counted. Estonia and Arizona have used this technique successfully. The 'last vote counts' seems like an obvious and plausible solution to many, but some experts continue to highlight coercion as a major issue with Internet voting.

Another approach to increasing the security of messages or votes is the use of two factor authentication (2FA). 2FA requires an additional piece of authentication in addition to a username and password. The username and password in a single factor authentication is information you know. 2FA supplements what you know with what you have. The things you can have for 2FA include a key fob carried in one's pocket, a digital certificate installed on a user's computer, a fingerprint, or retina scan to name a few common examples.

Charles Schwab, a provider of securities, brokerage, banking, money management, and financial advisory services, offers customers a key fob containing an LCD display. To log in securely to your Schwab account, you enter your username and password (what you know), but then the login page asks for the number displayed on the key fob (what you have). The key fob number changes every 60 seconds. After you enter the number, the Schwab server confirms the number is what it expected based on your identity. An alternative to a key fob is a smartphone. On my iPhone, I have an app called Authy. Authy can be connected to multiple apps and it generates a random number the apps expect. I use Authy with a number of other apps including my Coinbase digital wallet for Bitcoin, Evernote, and my Wordpress blog.

With two factor authentication and a strict password policy the likelihood of an imposter gaining access to your financial account or to cast your vote on an Internet server is highly unlikely. However, in addition to the concern about accurate authentication, there are other cybersecurity issues.

Breaches

Breaches of servers connected to the Internet in areas other than the voting process have emerged as a significant security concern. However, in my research, I found no cases of election servers being breached. There was the significant case of the Washington, D.C. voting pilot where the IT department failed to configure a strong password to protect the network router, leaving it plugged in, un-configured, and relying on the default set-up password—actually a simple unforced error. Jake Kouns, co-founder and President of the Open Security Foundation which oversees the operations of the Open Source Vulnerability Database, tracks data breaches in his DatalossDB.org blog. He reported 2015 had an all-time high 3,930 breaches of servers which exposed more than 736 million records. Forty-one percent of the servers and sixty-five percent of the records were in the U.S. None were election servers. Kouns said, "Email addresses, passwords and usernames were exposed in 38% of reported incidents. Passwords were the most sought after data to steal." Kouns said, "This is especially troubling since a high percentage of users pick a single password and use it on all their accounts both personal and work related." While weak passwords represent a security risk, there are numerous tools available to create and manage strong passwords.

Clearly, a strong password and 2FA is essential to prevent a brute force attack against one's online account. However, even with 2FA it is possible to breach a systems' security if SSL is improperly configured. Hackers understand encryption technology too. There have been a number of high-profile security breaches caused by improperly configured SSL based web servers. For example, a known vulnerability in the older SSL protocol allows hackers to break the encryption which otherwise would protect sensitive data. For this reason, it is imperative for organizations to be vigilant with best practices, such as enforcing the newer TLS protocol and disabling the legacy protocols altogether. Security best practices also include regularly applying security updates to prevent susceptibility to emerging threats when they are discovered.

A study of 2015 breaches was done by the Online Trust Alliance, a Bellevue, Washington charitable organization with the mission to enhance online trust and promote innovation and the vitality of the Internet. Its results were released January, 2016. It reported 91% of the data breaches occurring from January to August of 2015 could have been easily prevented using simple and well established security practices. One of the most important security practices is regularly applying software patches which can stop breaches of servers. As mentioned in chapter 2, this important practice is not followed on many voting machine servers because the voting machine software is out of date and no longer supported. The statistics about server breaches applies to servers connected to the Internet, but not election servers. The concern security experts raise is theoretical. Many of them believe if you had Internet voting, there would need to be election servers connected to the Internet which would create the risk of breaches. I conclude breaches are not to be ignored, but they are manageable if good security practices are followed.

Koshevoy Dmitry, author of a website about rules and tips for creating strong and secure passwords, wrote, "The most common password is the word 'password'." A server connected to the Internet must follow strict security policies including the requirement for strong passwords. The physical environment of the server room or datacenter also must be secure and inspected regularly.

Employees should be reminded to locate their password information in a different place than a stick-on memo on their PC screen or under their mouse pad.

Distributed Denial of Service Attacks

One of the most feared cybersecurity threats is from a Distributed Denial of Service Attack (DDoS). This is a coordinated attack in which many compromised systems, typically infected with a Trojan horse virus, are remotely commanded to repeatedly make requests to a single system thus overwhelming the system's resources and causing a denial of service to legitimate users.

A theoretical example may help clarify the meaning of a DDoS attack. Suppose a major U.S. state had an Internet voting server set up for a Presidential general election. The state is considered a swing state, meaning the state vote is so important it could determine the national outcome. Further assume a country unfriendly to America wanted to be sure a certain candidate was elected. That country could engage a group of hackers to develop a DDoS attack.

In our example, let's assume the state election officials contracted with an Internet voting company to provide an online election service which would be open to eligible voters for 12 hours on the day of the election. The eligible voter population of the state is 12,000,000. To handle this capacity, the voting server would need to be able to handle one million votes per hour. It would be 16,667 votes per minute or 278 votes per second. Since the voting would not likely take place on an even basis during the 12 hour period, the election officials decided to specify to the Internet voting company to ensure the system could handle a minimum of 1,000 votes per second.

Meanwhile, the hackers were busy planning the attack. First, they designed a Trojan horse virus. The term Trojan horse comes from a Greek story about the Trojan War. The Greeks built a giant wooden horse and presented it to the Trojans, making it look like a gift. After the Trojans dragged the horse inside their city walls, Greek soldiers exited the horse's hollow belly and opened the city gates. Greek soldiers were then able to swarm in and capture Troy. [307] The hackers' Trojan horse is made from software, not wood. The software is a virus, meaning it can have a detrimental effect on a computer such as erasing data or performing inappropriate actions. In this case, the virus would have caused the voter's computer to visit the state's election server and attempt to login with a random user ID and password.

The virus would not have been successful in logging in to the state's election server, but it would have been successful in using a small amount of the server's resources to look at the login and password and determine if they were legitimate. A single occurrence of the virus would not be a problem, but if the hackers could get the virus on millions of voter computers, and all of those computers could be commanded to attack the same election server or servers at the same time, it could cause the servers to become overwhelmed and not be able to provide service to legitimate voters. This is why the attack is called a Distributed Denial of Service.

In our hypothetical example, the Trojan horse virus the hackers designed was stored on the hackers' server. The hackers sent an email to millions of unsuspecting voters advertising a special service to make sure the voter's computer was ready to be used for voting. "Click here for a free checkup to make sure your computer is ready for election day." The email was sent to 10 million voters and only one percent, 100,000 voters clicked on the link, which in turn caused a copy of the virus to be copied from the hackers' server to the voter's computer. The 100,000 unsuspecting voters were not aware the virus was on their computer, but they now became part of a distributed network of computers which were prepared to launch attacks. When election day arrived, the viruses went into action. As soon as the election began, the 100,000 viruses began making continuous requests to the state's server which was designed to handle only 1,000 requests per second. The server would have been overwhelmed and effectively shut down. The votes of Internet voters would not have been counted. Voters might give up on voting, but others may have sought alternative ways to vote.

Some voters would go to their local polling place. Voters would not have time to follow a paper absentee ballot process. If the state had a system to deliver votes remotely by allowing the voter to download a PDF ballot, vote, and return it by email, fax, or upload it to a web portal, the votes could be counted. If the state did not plan for this alternate method, many votes would be lost. At a minimum, the state's voting process would be significantly disrupted. If the unfriendly country behind the hackers had wider aims, it would be possible there could be DDoS attacks against all the swing states. DDoS attacks are one of the cybersecurity concerns which worry security experts the most.

The scenario I described is one of the many forms a DDoS attack can take. The scenario is hypothetical and theoretical, but it is possible. Fortunately, it is also possible to plan ahead and thwart DDoS attacks. There are two basic approaches to protecting against a DDoS attack. One method is to add significant, but temporary capacity. This can be an expensive solution if it is needed 7x24x365 days. In the case of Internet voting, the window of time is much shorter, and 10X, 100X, or even more capacity can be sufficient to sustain an attack. If the capacity is present, the attack has no consequence. All of the login attempts are handled normally, and the legitimate ones are allowed access to the voting server.

The second defense to a DDoS attack is to prevent illegitimate requests from infected systems getting into the voting server. This can be done with specialized hardware devices which are connected to the Internet and to the voting server. The hardware device acts as a first line of defense. It inspects the contents of the incoming message and determines if it is legitimate based on where it came from and how the request is structured. Numerous vendors, including Akamai, Arbor Networks, Barracuda, Cisco, Radware, and Verizon have sophisticated solutions specifically designed to protect against DDoS attacks. The Arizona Democratic Party in March 2000 experienced two types of cybersecurity attacks, brute force password guessing attempts and DDoS. Both attacks were thwarted successfully.

End-to-end Verifiable Internet Voting

Dr. David Dill, former Professor of Computer Science at Stanford University, and now on leave as Chief Scientist at LocusPoint Networks, an early stage wireless communications company, is strongly opposed to Internet voting. He makes a fair contrast with e-commerce. "Voting is just different", he said. "If someone steals your credit card, you will know it, even though it may be much later when your billing statement arrives. If someone steals your vote, you may not ever know it."[308] An important characteristic for an accurate voting system is the need for verifiability. Dr. Dill and other anti-Internet voting activists say it is not optional. Voting must be verifiable, and the only way to make it verifiable, he believes, is to have a paper receipt.

Verified voting is simple in concept. It allows voters to verify the recorded vote was what they intended. It allows a subsequent audit to confirm the vote tally equals the total votes cast. To put verifiability in perspective, consider the following two existing methods. In the first case, a vote cast at a voting machine capable of printing a receipt. The voter can look at the receipt and verify their vote was as intended. This method requires the voter to trust the voting machine has not been hacked or modified by the manufacturer to print a receipt which is different from the vote actually recorded A second method is to vote on a touchscreen with no receipt. This second method is not verifiable and would be much harder to trust. The Direct Recording Electronic voting systems, called DREs, without paper receipts are used in seven states including Florida, Indiana, Kentucky, Pennsylvania, Tennessee, Texas, and Virginia. I believe it is likely these states selected the DREs without paper receipt printing capability because of the lower cost. Although the authors of *Broken Ballots* pointed out a number of theoretical security exposures with these machines, I could not find any instances where problems arose.

Different groups interested in the voting process hold varied opinions on what makes a voting system verifiable. Verified Voting, based in Carlsbad, California, describes itself as a non-partisan, non-profit organization which advocates for legislation and regulation that promotes accuracy, transparency and verifiability of elections. Verified Voting believes as their first principle for a voting machine with verified voting capability, "It should use human-readable marks on paper as the official record of voter preferences and as the official medium to store votes." Dr. David Dill, founder of Verified Voting, does believe there could be a way to make Internet voting verifiable, but he thinks the result would weaken privacy and make the voting process too complicated.[309] He gives as an example, "If an Internet voting system was designed to email a ballot receipt to a voter, the sent email could be accessible by the sender, thereby compromising the voter's privacy."[310] Although I respect Dr. Dill's points of view, I believe his objections can be overcome with new technology from companies such as Everyone Counts, Inc., Follow My Vote, Helios Voting Systems, Smartmatic, and others.

Verified Voting colleagues and other voting experts I have interviewed see end to end verifiability as an essential part of an American election system. An end to end voting system must provide the voter with certain assurances. The following list is what I believe a voter should expect from a voting system built with an election attitude.

1) Easy registration and update process
2) Multiple ballot formats available: mail, email, website, or online via the Internet
3) Ability to select your preferred method, in person, by mail, email, fax, or via the Internet
4) Guaranteed vote recording

5) Guaranteed vote counting as it was recorded
6) Individual verification vote was recorded as cast

The U.S. Vote Foundation is a 501(c)(3) nonprofit, nonpartisan, public charity based in Arlington, Virginia. The Foundation provides absentee ballot request and voter registration services for all U.S. voters in all states at home and abroad. It initiated a project called The Future of Voting: End-to-end Verifiable Internet Voting (E2E-VIV). The 127 page Report, published in 2015, included five key recommendations:

1) Any public elections conducted over the Internet must be end-to-end verifiable.
2) No Internet voting system of any kind should be used for public elections before end-to-end verifiable in-person voting systems have been widely deployed and experience has been gained from their use.
3) End-to-end verifiable systems must be designed, constructed, verified, certified, operated, and supported according to the most rigorous engineering requirements of mission and safety critical systems.
4) End-to-End Verifiable Internet Voting systems must be usable and accessible.
5) Many challenges remain in building a usable, reliable, and secure End-to-End Verifiable Internet Voting system. They must be overcome before using Internet voting for public elections. Research and development efforts toward overcoming those challenges should continue.[311]

The footnote to the recommendations says, "It is currently unclear whether it is possible to construct an E2E-VIV system that fulfills the set of requirements contained in this report."[312] The recommendations are hard to dispute, but, to me, the requirements outlined are so stringent they may be impossible to implement. A typical report of this nature would include recommendations grounded in reality, mitigating alternatives, and recommendations to overcome the challenges. The technical team and advisory council for the project consisted of 19 members. Although the organizations are separate, eight members of the U.S. Vote Foundation were board members or advisory board members at Verified Voting.

I believe the E2E-VIV Report is comprehensive but idealistic. If a similar approach to e-commerce had been taken in the early 1990s, and if a comparable organization to Verified Voting had existed lobbying against e-commerce, Amazon may not have been developed. E-commerce started small and continuously improved its capability. An election attitude could enable Internet voting to start small and likewise continuously evolve.

The other concern I have about the E2E-VIV Report is it recommends a system which is potentially impossible to develop with the current level of Internet voting technology. The E2E-VIV system is clearly better. However, I believe the current level of Internet voting, if implemented through pilots and constant improvements could be much better than the partly unverifiable system we have today.

In addition to the DRE voting machines with no paper receipt, there are questions about the millions of votes cast by mail. For example, Oregon has voting by mail. When an Oregon voter fills out a ballot and places it in a USPS mailbox, there is no verifiability. The voter doesn't even know if the ballot gets to the election center. A postal worker could be bribed to throw ballots coming from certain voting precincts in a dumpster, or could lose some by mistake.

Despite this, Verified Voting believes paper is essential to a verifiable voting system. Other computer science experts disagree. Josh Benaloh, a senior cryptographer at Microsoft Research, where he works on data security, privacy, and verifiable election technologies, disagrees. He earned an S.B. from MIT, and M.S., M. Phil., and Ph. D. degrees from Yale University. His 1987 doctoral dissertation introduced a new paradigm for verifiable secret-ballot elections. Dr. Benaloh was part of a technical team that studied the future of voting and the viability of voting using the Internet. He sees end-to-end verifiable voting as critical to good voting practice and essential to any responsible Internet voting system, but he does not feel this requires using paper voting receipts. Since the anti-Internet voting activists believe the paper receipt is critical, I asked Dr. Benaloh his opinion. He said,

> We want our election systems to be verifiable, and paper is a useful medium that can help support verifiability. But paper and verifiability are not the same thing and should not be confused. There are very weak paper-based election systems with exceptionally poor verifiability, and there are very strong paperless election systems with excellent verifiability. Paper is not an essential ingredient of election verifiability.[313]

Conclusion

Strong cybersecurity is a critical factor for a successful and trusted Internet voting system. I do not believe the difficulties in developing strong cybersecurity is a reason to not pursue the adoption of Internet voting. Federal, state, and local election officials should work with security experts to develop Internet voting pilots. Internet security requires more than technology. The voting policies and procedures must be airtight. The server connected to the Internet must follow strict security policies, which among other things must require strong passwords and ideally require two factor authentication.

Professional services are available from many reputable companies to provide assistance in all aspects of Internet security. These include developing security policies and operational procedures. If properly implemented, such policies and procedures can greatly reduce risk from security breaches or DDoS attacks. Unfortunately, cost prohibits many election officials from such efforts despite the risk incurred. In many cases, a breach or attack can cost much more than it would to implement proper security in the first place. Strong cybersecurity is a key component to adopting a new election attitude.

CHAPTER 6

Other Challenges to Internet Voting

The current system of American voting faces many challenges including inaccurate registration data, lost ballots, inaccurate counting of votes, and broken voting machines. Use of the Internet to improve the voting systems does present cybersecurity challenges, but I believe they are surmountable. The following sections describe some additional challenges to creating an improved system of voting.

Voter Registration

A significant challenge for Internet voting occurs before voting begins. The challenge lies with problems in voter registration, in both the existing system of voting and in Internet voting trials. It was estimated up to two million voters were not able to vote in the Presidential elections of 2000 because of registration errors.[314] As demonstrated in the March 2016, Utah Republican Internet voting trial, there were thousands of citizens who wanted to vote online but could not due to registration errors.

Although registration procedures vary among the more than 10,000 voting jurisdictions countrywide[315], the role of the voter registration process is mainly the same. In order to vote, you need to be registered. Most states require pre-registration prior to election day. The vast majority of voter registrations occur by mail or via online voter registration. There is no confirmation process, as it is an honor system. When submitting and signing a voter registration form, the voter is asked to attest to the following, "Above information is true and correct". It is a felony to falsify registration information.

If you show an ID at the polling place with an incorrect address, you cannot vote. In some states, you can fill out a provisional ballot and if the registration issue is resolved in a few days, your vote will count, although it may be after the election is over. In the situation in Utah, there was no online process to file a provisional ballot. Voters were told to call a help line if there were any problems in the online voting process. However, if the problem was a discrepancy in the registration information, there was nothing the helpline could do.

There are several reasons for the problems with voter registration. The voter could have filled out a registration request incorrectly or entered incorrect information online. If a registration request was mailed to an election office, a member of the election staff could have entered the data into the database incorrectly. The required time to be registered prior to Election Day varies from state to state but, if the registration does not meet the required timeframe, the citizen cannot vote. In many states, registration must take place a month or more prior to the election. People who move from state to state often are not aware of the different state requirements. Elderly people who no longer drive often do not have a photo ID. In a *Scientific American* article "Fixing the Vote: Electronic Voting Machines Promise to Make Fixing Elections More Accurate Than Ever before, but Only If Certain Problems—with the Machines and the Wider Electoral Process—Are Rectified", Ted Selker, Visiting Scientist at the Center for Information Technology in Interest of Society at UC Berkeley said, "Registration problems prevent millions of citizens from voting."[316] On the positive side, online registration via the Internet is growing rapidly. As of May 4, 2016, 31 states plus the District of Columbia offered online voter registration.[317] Five additional states have passed legislation to create online voter registration systems, but have not implemented them yet.

Validation of voter registration information is performed by comparing it to the voter's driver's license or other state-issued identification cards. If a person entered his or her name with a middle name when obtaining a driver license or for other state transaction, the same name must be used for voter registration. When the information does not match, such as when the registration application shows a middle initial instead of a middle name, the application is sent to officials for further review or action. Online registration can be a boost for voter participation by reducing the number of voters who are rejected. Data can be entered by the voter and verified in real time.

Offsetting Registration Benefits

Online registration also has the potential for significant cost savings. A case study in Arizona showed a reduction in registration costs from 83 cents per paper registration to 3 cents per online registration.[318] The cost to implement online registration systems in some states was absorbed easily within existing budgets. The funds from the Help America Vote Act have been used in some states to implement online voter registration. Although the savings potential has been shown to be real, moving to online registration requires vision, leadership, and funding.

Online registration is one component of e-government. The U.S. ranks number seven in the world as an e-government leader, based on The United Nations 2014 E-Government Survey.[319] The survey presents a systematic assessment of how well the 193 Member States of the United Nations use information and communication technologies to transform the public sector by enhancing efficiency, effectiveness, transparency, accountability, access to public services, and citizen participation. The six countries which rank higher than the U.S. include: 1) The Republic of Korea, 2) Australia, 3) Singapore, 4) France, 5) Netherlands, and 6) Japan.

Adoption of e-government among the U.S. states varies widely. In its comprehensive 2014 Digital States Survey, the Center for Digital Government evaluated the digital technology practices in all 50 states. Grades from A to D were assigned based on quantifiable results in better serving citizens and streamlining operations. Compared to the results of the 2012 survey, grades improved in 21 states, declined in 12 and stayed even in 17.[320] Eight states earned top grades: Connecticut, Georgia, Michigan, Missouri, Ohio, Pennsylvania, Utah, and Virginia. The states receiving a C or lower grade included Alabama, Alaska, Florida, Nevada, New Hampshire, Oklahoma, Rhode Island, and Wyoming. The rankings do not specifically highlight performance at voter registration.

Current and accurate registration data about voters sets the stage for the actual voting. However, even if all eligible citizens were properly registered, other challenges need to be solved prior to implementing Internet voting.

Election Officials Training

Internet voting represents a major shift in the process of how elections are conducted. Election officials will need to be trained in the new processes. If they are not trained prior to implementation of Internet voting, problems could arise. A similar training challenge existed when healthcare providers began to implement electronic health records. The clipboard, manila folders, and fax machines had been the lingua franca in healthcare for decades. E-prescribing was another change in process which required major staff re-training. It was adopted at a very slow pace until the federal, state, and local provided billions of dollars of incentives. The incentives worked. More than half of prescriptions now are created electronically resulting in lower medication errors and improved patient safety.[321] Like physicians facing the change to electronic prescribing, election officials at the state and county levels will need training to implement Internet voting. It will be essential for vendors to develop Internet voting systems which are easy to use and to provide training programs to election officials.

Privacy at Home

A frequent objection by Internet voting critics is the lack of privacy and the possibility of coercion. I think Internet voting would provide more privacy, not less. When I curl up in a chair or on a park bench and review communications, financial, or healthcare data, I feel completely private. In many current voting places during a closed primary, you are asked which party you belong to so you will get the correct ballot. This can take place where anyone can hear you say which party you belong to, which certainly isn't private.

While I believe there are advantages to being able to vote from the privacy of one's home, some are concerned there could be a danger. A friend, family member, or visitor may coerce or bribe a voter to cast an unintended ballot. In an extreme and highly unlikely case, one or more persons could surround the voter and threaten harm unless a certain vote is cast. Fortunately, there is a simple solution to these problems. After the person or persons making the threat have departed, the voter could cast his or her vote a second time. The voter could actually vote multiple times up until the time the voting period is over. The last vote cast would be the one which counts. Estonia and Arizona have used this method successfully. A voter under duress or perceiving a threat could go to the local library and cast the ballot there. Some critics believe voting outside the polling place is not secure against coercion by those who buy last minute votes. I believe this is a minimal risk compared to the many flaws in our current system.

The Status Quo

When Internet voting is introduced, it will represent a major change from the way voting works today. Most changes of this magnitude face resistance by those interested in preserving the status quo. "Follow the money" is a catchphrase said to have originated in William Goldman's screenplay for the 1976 film *All the President's Men*.[322] Current use of the Internet has disrupted multiple industries, and in each case I believe the flow of money has been a major factor.

For example, Apple's iPod and iTunes were the beginning of the demise of music tapes and CDs, which in their turn had caused the demise of vinyl records. Since Apple has become more aggressive in the movie business they are beginning to disrupt the movie theatre status quo. Money has moved from traditional publishers and broadcasters to a new business model Apple calls services. Apple reported revenue of $8.9 billion from music, apps, and movies during the last quarter of 2015.[323] The company does not break out the details of its services revenue, but they have reported 13 million Apple Music subscribers.[324] At $10 per month, the annualized revenue would be $1.6 billion. In 1997, Apple's revenue from music was zero.

There are other examples of major changes disrupting the status quo. Amazon disrupted the book industry with the Kindle which changed how many people feel about reading a physical book. Consumers began to purchase books from Amazon on-line or on Kindle rather than buying hard copy books from a traditional book store.

More recently, Uber, the American multinational online transportation network company headquartered in San Francisco, California, has faced strong resistance from local taxi commissions. Millions of consumers consider Uber the smartest way to get around. One tap on your smartphone and a car comes directly to you. You enter where you want to go and the driver sees it on his or her smartphone. Payment is completely cashless using the credit card you have on file with Uber. Taxi operators in New York pay large fees to get a medallion from the taxi commission authorizing them to operate.

Airbnb, a San Francisco, California based private company, provides an online community marketplace for people to list, discover, and book lodging accommodations around the world. A consumer may be looking for an apartment for a night, a castle for a week, or a villa for a month. Airbnb operates in more than 34,000 cities and 191 countries. Consumers like the service, but the company has raised concerns from hotel operators and municipal tax collectors.

Bitcoin, the digital currency described in chapter 4, has raised concern from banks and money transfer companies which collect large transaction fees which may not be justified in a world of digital currencies. Bitcoin is now accepted by 100,000 merchants worldwide.[325]

In all of these examples, the issue revolves around money. Disrupting the status quo disrupts the allocation of money, and usually means money moves from old to new companies. In all of the cases, those benefiting from the status quo have resisted change.

The Voting Machine Industry

The industry serving governmental voting jurisdictions consists mostly of traditional voting machine companies. The voting machine industry has had a checkered past. The authors of *Broken Ballots* cited numerous cases of monopolization, corruption, and conflicts of interest.[326]

At one point, there were 19 voting machine companies listed in the Federal Election Commission Buyers Guide, but the guide is no longer available. Through a series of mergers, acquisitions, and business failures, the voting machine industry currently is dominated by the three companies. All three companies are privately held and do not disclose their revenue or profits.

Dominion Voting Systems Corporation is based in Toronto, Canada. It sells electronic voting and tabulating hardware around the world. In May 2010, Dominion acquired Premier Election Solutions, formerly Diebold Election Systems, from Election Systems & Software. They just had acquired Premier Election Solutions from Diebold, but were required by the United States Department of Justice to sell Premier Election Solutions for anti-trust concerns.

Election Systems & Software, based in Omaha, Nebraska, is the giant of the voting machine industry. In addition to a line of hardware products, the company provides equipment rental, print services, maintenance services, ballot management services, election support, professional services, and voter registration mailing services. The company's equipment, software, and services are used by municipalities and counties throughout the U.S.

Hart InterCivic, based in Austin, Texas, has been working with election professionals for more than 100 years. The company makes a wide range of voting machine hardware and services. Its election services include consultation, training, professional services, preventative maintenance, and ballot production services. The company claims its mission is to help advance democracy one election at a time.[327]

A review of the websites of these three companies reveals they all claim to be innovative. However, in my opinion, when you look at their products and services, they are basically refinements of decades old technology. Although it may take a decade, I believe Internet voting revenue will replace most of the existing revenue of these companies. In the future, voting industry revenue will come from software and services.

The question is whether these companies will reinvent themselves and become leaders in the future or whether they will not change and cling to the status quo. If they choose to lead, they will have significant advantages. They have long standing relationships with government election professionals and have employees who understand the voting process. The music and publishing industries waited too long to embrace the Internet and newcomers such as Apple and Amazon took the lead, and the revenue. It is possible new companies will do the same thing to the election industry.

Incumbent Politicians

There are different views concerning who benefits the most from high voter turnouts. Thomas Hansford, Associate Professor of Political Science, University of California and Brad T. Gomez, Associate Professor of Political Science, Florida State University studied this question. In their 2010 paper, "Estimating the Electoral Effects of Voter Turnout", the researchers concluded, "High turnout elections portend partisan change, anti-incumbency tendencies, and generally less predictable consequences."[328]

I believe Internet voting will bring more voters to the polls, and higher voting turnout will not benefit incumbents. Washington Post's Amber Phillips investigated the relationship between politics and the adoption of Internet voting. She said, "Politicians want to keep their jobs, and one of the best ways to do that is to avoid massive turnout that could get them in trouble -- especially should any negative headlines come their way before Election Day."[329]

The Center for Public Integrity, a nonprofit, nonpartisan organization which does investigations and analyses of public service, government accountability, and ethics related issues said,

Being a member of Congress remains a surprisingly sweet gig. In addition to the power to shape policy and public discourse, legislators get great health care and retirement benefits, hefty salaries with annual cost of living increases and the incumbency-boosting ability to blanket constituents with mail touting their achievements. [330]

Joe Mohen agrees. He is an entrepreneur best known as co-founder and CEO of election.com, the company which ran a successful trial of Internet voting for the Arizona Democratic Primary in March 2000. He believes incumbents are very focused on staying in office to preserve the perks they receive.

Mohen said, "Politicians get reelected more than 80% of the time."[331] According to The Center for Responsive Politics, a non-profit, nonpartisan research group based in Washington, D.C., his estimate is low. Between 1964 and 2014, the reelection rate averaged 93%.[332] Mohen believes the reelection rate would drop to 50% if Internet voting was implemented nationwide. The 50% number is hard to prove, but I believe Mohen's rationale is logical. He said, "With Internet voting, it will be much easier to vote and participation will rise significantly. If more people vote, those who are dissatisfied with the incumbents will have a stronger voice."

In August 2015, a Gallup poll showed Congress approval fell to 14% from 17%.[333] As of May 23, 2016, a RealClearPolitics average of six surveys put the approval rating at 13.3% with a disapproval rating of 78.2%.[334] In my research, I found no current congressional politicians from the Democrat or Republican party pushing for the adoption of Internet voting. Despite the many benefits to citizens of an easier, more convenient voting system, there appears to be no political will to change the American system of voting.

The 'It Just Can't Be Done' Attitude

The strongest challenge to Internet voting comes from a small, highly influential, and knowledgeable group of anti-Internet voting activists. During the early to mid 1990s, the attitude of many technologists and business people concerning potential uses for the Internet was very different from what it is today. I attended a conference in Paris, France in 1995 where Bill Gates was the keynote speaker. He said that the Internet had no place in business because it was too slow, insecure, and unreliable. At the same time, I also met with banking and insurance executives who told me they would never connect their firms to the Internet. Even IBM computer scientists were skeptical of the Internet. One IBM Fellow, with a PhD in computer science, told me it was not possible to perform transactions on the Internet. He said, "It just can't be done."

IBMs proprietary networking software at the time, Systems Network Architecture, used very sophisticated software, developed in the mid 1970s, called Virtual Telecommunications Access Method, known as VTAM. Most large enterprises in the world at the time the Internet was emerging used IBM's VTAM. VTAM provided the basis for a deterministic network. This meant the sender and receiver of a digital packet of information could determine with certainty exactly the state of the information packet. In other words, the sender and receiver knew exactly where the packet of information was. When the packet of information arrived at the destination, the sender and receiver got a confirmation.

During the early 1990s, as the Internet was beginning to emerge into the business world, computer engineers realized the Internet was not a deterministic network like VTAM. Senders and receivers had no way to confirm if an information packet had arrived at its destination. This is why the IBM Fellow believed it would be impossible to perform transactions using the Internet. There was no state built into how the Internet worked. This meant if you visited a website, the website would not know you visited, so if you came back again it would not recognize you. Remembering you had visited and what you were doing on the site when you visited is called the "state" of your visit. Mainframe systems, with VTAM, had this capability. The Internet, prior to cookies, did not.

Netscape Communications, founded in Mountain View, California and best known for its web browser, Netscape Navigator, set out in the early 1990s to enable companies to use Internet webservers to perform transactions many believed only IBM mainframes with VTAM could perform. Netscape had a vision for the Internet which went beyond the limitations the computer scientists at IBM accepted. The Internet's lack of state would be solved by the invention in 1994 of the cookie by Netscape Internet pioneer Lou Montulli.[335] A cookie is a small file containing a piece of text. The cookie file could contain a user ID. When a user visited a website, the webserver would write the small cookie file on the user's computer. When a user visited the website a few seconds later or months later, the webserver would look on the user's computer and if it found the cookie, it would know the identity of the returning visitor. In other words, the cookie gave the Internet the ability to do things previously only possible with mainframe software.

The cookie is a simple concept, but it enabled Internet pioneers to eventually build websites which could do anything IBM's mainframes and VTAM could do. The implementation of the cookie was not a remake of the Internet. The 24 year old Netscape software engineer did not have blinders on. He knew what he was trying to accomplish and he invented a solution. It was a small tweak inspired by a vision. The Internet approach to handling transactions was not nearly as robust as IBM's approach at the beginning, but the Internet evolved rapidly. IBM adopted Internet technology in 1995, and within a few years, incorporated it into all of its hardware and software solutions.

There have been countless ideas where one or more pundits said, "It just can't be done." In 1972, a study about world dynamics was sponsored by The Club of Rome, a global think tank that deals with a variety of international political issues. The study resulted in a book, *The Limits to Growth: A Report for the Club of Rome's Project on the Predicament of Mankind.*[336] This book was my introduction to brilliant people's pessimism. The book presented a simulation model based on five variables: world population, industrialization, pollution, food production, and resource depletion. The model was developed by Jay Wright Forrester, an American pioneering computer engineer and systems scientist. He was a professor at the MIT Sloan School of Management and is known as the founder of system dynamics.[337]

The five variables in the study were considered to grow exponentially, while the ability of technology to increase resources availability was believed to be linear. The initial simulation showed the world would collapse by the beginning of the 21st century because there would be too many people, insufficient production, overwhelming pollution, a shortage of food, and a depletion of critical resources. The authors explored the possibility of breakthroughs to avoid the collapse. After considering the most optimistic scenarios imaginable, the conclusion was essentially the same. The world could collapse. Needless to say, the world did not collapse. Brilliant as they were, the researchers could not see the future breakthroughs which would occur. In other words, they thought, "It just can't be done."

Some computer scientists have become anti-Internet voting activists and share a similar attitude toward Internet voting. "It just can't be done." Following are a few examples of this anti-Internet voting activist attitude:

> It's going to be decades, if ever, before the technology used for security is at the point where online voting can be done with confidence. There's just so much that can go wrong, and the need for it is not nearly so pressing as the risk (2016).[338]

> J. Alex Halderman, Ph.D., Assistant Professor of Computer Science and Engineering, University of Michigan and member Board of Advisors at Verified Voting.

Our goal is to convince you that secure Internet voting is unachievable for the foreseeable future and therefore, we sincerely hope, not inevitable.

"Internet Voting in the U.S." (2012) by Barbara Simons, Ph.D. and Douglas W. Jones, Ph.D.[339] Simons, Chair of the Board of Directors of Verified Voting and member of the Board of Advisers of the U.S. Election Assistance Commission. Douglas W. Jones, Professor of Computer Science, University of Iowa and member Board of Advisors at Verified Voting.

Internet voting is a nonstarter. You can't control the security of the platform. The app you're using, the operating system on your phone, the servers your data will cross en route to their destination, there are just too many openings for hacker interference (2016).[340]

Aviel D. Rubin, Ph.D., Professor of Computer Science, Johns Hopkins University and member Board of Advisors at Verified Voting.

I have not yet seen anyone come up with any way to address the security problems we identified with Internet voting and I believe it would require either some new breakthrough or a wholesale change to our computing infrastructure (2011).[341]

David Wagner, Professor, Computer Science Division, University of California, Berkeley.

The dissenting anti-Internet voting activists, who effectively torpedoed the military and overseas citizens Internet voting expansion pilot, hold Ph.D. degrees and have very impressive backgrounds. Two of them, Barbara Simons and David Jefferson are board members at Verified Voting.[342] Aviel D. Rubin is a member of the Verified Voting Board of Advisors. The fourth, David Wagner, is Professor at Berkeley Electrical Engineering & Computer Sciences.

Verified Voting

Carlsbad, California based Verified Voting is comprised of two separate organizations. Verified Voting Foundation is a 501(c)(3) nonprofit educational organization founded in 2003 by Dr. Dill. VerifiedVoting.org is a 501(c)(4) nonprofit lobbying organization formed at about the same time. The two organizations engage in many of the same activities, but the IRS requires the lobbying activities be funded separately. The two organizations have nearly identical mission statements.

> We believe the integrity and strength of our democracy relies on citizens' trust that each vote be counted as cast. Our primary concern lies in ensuring that the means for verifying election outcomes are in place and used for that purpose. We also focus on the reliability and security of voting systems. We connect those who are making and implementing policy that shapes how we vote to those who understand the particular risks associated with the emerging digital landscape, particularly online and electronic voting.[343]

Verified Voting has significant breadth and depth of experience on voting and voting rights. The staff and board members provide education and advice to election officials, voter advocates, lawmakers, technologists, researchers, and the media. A major focus of Verified Voting is to ensure auditable systems are in place and ensuring audits are conducted. They actively seek to eliminate or greatly reduce the use of systems which cannot be audited. They include the use of the Internet in voting to be among the systems which cannot be audited.

In an interview in 2016 with Pamela Smith, President of Verified Voting, she explained that Verified Voting provides information and public testimony on voting issues at federal and state levels throughout the U.S.[344] Ms. Smith is co-editor of the "Principles and Best Practices in Post Election Audits," co-author of "Counting Votes 2012: A State by State Look at Election Preparedness", and is a contributing author for "Confirming Elections: Creating Confidence and Integrity through Election Auditing".

I asked Ms. Smith if Verified Voting was biased against Internet voting. She would not use the term biased but agreed the organization considers Internet voting to be risky, not verifiable, and not ready for widespread use.[345] She acknowledged the current system has many flaws, but believes the focus should be to fix the current system rather than introduce what Verified Voting considers to be unproven technology. Verified Voting endorses what Los Angeles County and Travis County are doing to specify improved voting systems, but not the use of the Internet.

The publicly available tax returns for the two Verified Voting organizations reveal they had income of approximately $4.6 million during 2004-2013 and expenditures on program activities of approximately $2.5 million. Almost 90% of the income is collected by the educational organization. The source of the funding is mostly grants from non-profit foundations which have an interest in American democracy and the election process. There are no members of Verified Voting but they do use mailing lists to solicit donations from individuals. Ms. Smith assured me that the voting machine industry is not among the donors to Verified Voting or its Foundation.

I take Verified Voting's stated goals and mission at face value. I believe they are strongly committed to helping assure American democracy is protected with auditable voting processes. When it comes to Internet voting proposals or even discussions about the topic, the voice of at least one of the board members or board advisory members is present. With 9 board members and 31 advisory board members, it is a formidable group. Their papers and sound bites concerning the dangers of Internet voting are widely circulated. Their messages about the dangers of Internet voting are consistently negative. Based on discussions with people directly associated with Verified Voting, election officials who have talked to them, and quotations attributed to them, I conclude Verified Voting's unstated goal is to stop Internet voting in its tracks. The elite anti-Internet voting activists actively lobby and speak out in a manner which often frightens politicians and election officials from even considering Internet voting pilots.

I believe Verified Voting's message is a response to their concern voting officials or politicians might perceive that citizens want Internet voting. They further believe claims by boastful vendors that Internet voting is ready are not valid. I understand the concern raised by some voting systems administrative staff who may not have the background or skills to implement secure Internet voting today. They may not have the funds to hire the necessary skills. Despite my understanding of the Verified Voting exploits to criticize Internet voting pilots, I have some concerns about how they are displaying their critiques.

There is little acknowledgement in Verified Voting's publications or quotes about how Internet voting would compare to the dire situation of the current system of antiquated, insecure voting machines. Comparisons are made between Internet voting of today and a perfect Internet voting system in the future. The concerns raised about Internet voting are legitimate concerns, but are theoretical and not supported with statistical analysis showing the probability of their concerns actually occurring. Other than the End to End Verifiable Internet Voting paper in which Verified Voting board and advisory members actively participated, I could not find papers with specific constructive suggestions for how to make Internet voting pilots more successful. Neither could I discover any suggested strategies for mitigating the concerns they raise. Although solutions are not their primary responsibility, it would be helpful if they used their incredible talent pool to collaborate on developing creative solutions.

I would like to see more discussion from Verified Voting on their research about Internet voting. I have concerns about the approach some of the board and advisory board members of Verified Voting have used to undermine Internet voting trials. While finding weaknesses can be helpful, I found the communications following the Estonia and the District of Columbia pilot projects on Internet voting to be more destructive than constructive.

When I started to research this book, I did not expect to find one of the major challenges to introducing the use of the Internet into the voting process would come from computer scientists. Although I share some of the concerns raised by Verified Voting and others, I feel the challenges can be overcome. I agree with Ms. Smith when she said, "Let the research continue".[346]

Think Big, Act Bold, Start Simple, Iterate Fast

I believe there are two ways to consider the feasibility of Internet voting. One is the doom and gloom approach advocated by the anti-Internet voting activists. "Never is too soon," some say. Another view is to follow the kind of thinking the young Netscape programmer applied to make the Internet able to replace traditional networking. In the late 1990s, I developed a mantra which matches his approach. I believe it can enhance an election attitude. I called it Think Big, Act Bold, Start Simple, Iterate Fast.[347]

Think Big is about the potential to greatly increase voter participation and strengthen our democracy. I believe Internet voting has the potential to make these improvements.

Act Bold is what the Utah Republicans did in 2016. They took a calculated risk by trying Internet voting. They found they were able to enfranchise thousands of voters of all ages who were able to vote from home or remotely. Many voters were serving with the military or living and working abroad. Mormon missionaries voted from 45 countries.[348] Voters were able to reliably vote using the Internet.

Start Simple is the third element of the mantra, and perhaps most important. Healthcare.gov thought big, acted bold, but started big and initially failed big. A smaller start or a pilot project has a higher chance of success.

Iterate Fast is the path to ultimate success. Most multi-billion dollar Internet companies have followed this part of the mantra and continue to do so. The Internet voting proposal for military and overseas citizens was an excellent idea with broad support. The supporters started simple and had a successful pilot with just 84 voters. Unfortunately, the follow-on pilot designed for 100,000 was not permitted to proceed because of the strong voice of just four dissenters.

America is a big place with states bigger than many countries. A national election voting server would not be a good idea. However, a national blueprint for how Internet voting could work would be a great idea. Each state and its election jurisdictions could implement on their own schedule based on their unique needs and skills. The key is then to iterate fast based on what is learned. Estonia is not resting on its laurels. It is continually improving and strengthening its Internet voting system by refining processes, adopting new technology, and continuously reviewing how the system works.

A good starting point for how to think about Internet voting is a 2016 report from the Atlantic Council entitled, "Democracy Rebooted: The Future of Technology in Elections", written by Conny McCormack.[349] The Atlantic Council is a 501(c)(3) non-profit organization which promotes constructive leadership and engagement in international affairs based on the Atlantic Community's central role in meeting global challenges. The origins of the organization dates to the signing of the North Atlantic Treaty in 1949. The Council publishes authoritative papers and reports intended to shape policy choices and strategies to create a more secure and prosperous world.

Toomas Hendrik Ilves, President of Estonia, summed up Internet voting at an Atlantic Council conference as follows,

> In an era where citizens engage in everything from communication to education to leisure through technology, it is time to access how elections can become reflective of modern realities. Estonia has been the leader in implementing technology to strengthen our democracy. The Atlantic Council offers excellent advice for implementing modern elections and provides the international community recommendations for how countries can best use the latest technology in their elections.[350]

Another Atlantic Council report, written in 2014, is titled, "Online Voting: Rewards and Risks". The author, Peter Haynes, is a Nonresident Senior Fellow for the Atlantic Council's Strategic Foresight Initiative and Vice President of Product Strategy at Polyverse Corporation, a cybersecurity company. A summary of the report states,

> With the right, carefully chosen security considerations, online and e-voting could become more widespread. The report found that many of the technologies that handle online financial transactions could be applied to make e-voting and online voting a reality.[351]

The Report provides specific guidelines for how to create a secure Internet voting system. The Internet voting seeds are planted. Discussions are underway across the country among voting election officials. Innovative startup companies are working on developing new technologies to modernize the way we register and vote. Although the Internet is not perfect, and there are challenges which need to be addressed prior to adopting Internet voting, the path to an election attitude offers many advantages.

CHAPTER 7

Voting with an Election Attitude

E ven though Internet voting has some opponents, there are experts who see the potential benefits. Stephen Ansolabehere, Professor of Government at Harvard University, is an expert in public opinion and elections and he has published extensively on the subject of elections. He is a Truman Scholar (1982), Hoover National Fellow (1994), Carnegie Scholar (2000), and was inducted into the American Academy of Arts and Sciences in 2007. He directed the Caltech/MIT Voting Technology Project from its founding in 2000 through 2004.

Dr. Ansolabehere believes significant changes in the entire voting system, especially the voter registration, identification, and authentication processes, are required to realize the potential of full-scale online voting. He is optimistic such changes will occur and says online registration is, "...starting to snowball and become more widespread."[352] He continued, "By 2024 half of all people will be in jurisdictions where they can register online. Maybe sooner."[353] Although there have been some successful trials, Dr. Ansolabehere believes the ability to cast votes online is going to take more time.[354] However, he is one of the few experts who is optimistic Internet voting can be done securely. He said, "Online voting is securable and, although a bit cumbersome, there are some technology models which can provide secure online voting."[355] Dr. Ansolabehere also sees beyond the problems to the benefits. He added,

> The benefits of online voting are many. It would increase access for communities for whom the current system just doesn't work, especially

people with disabilities and overseas military personnel. It could make it much easier to run elections through the election office. Vote by mail in Oregon and Washington has totally changed election administration in those states. Those states' experiences are analogous to Internet voting. I can see online voting becoming the platform that replaces all absentee systems. By the middle of the next decade, the cultural objections to online voting will seem anachronistic.[356]

Conny McCormack is a recognized international election administration expert and consultant. She has spent 25 years in government service including as the Los Angeles County Registrar-Recorder/County Clerk, running elections for the largest election jurisdiction in the U.S. with 4.5 million voters. She is the author of "Democracy Rebooted: The Future of Technology in Elections", which takes a global look at the progress countries are making in the use of voting technology including Internet voting.[357] She believes the current model of paper-based voting systems in America is antiquated and unsustainable. In an interview, she said,

Voters are increasingly tech-savvy and our millennial voters virtually live online. They expect more when it comes to our voting systems and are incredulous at the archaic way we handle votes. The concept of making a mark on a piece of paper at a polling place or putting it in an envelope for the USPS to deliver is foreign to them.[358]

McCormack believes bottom-up demands from voters will put pressure on policymakers to consider Internet voting. She also said,

Now that voters in Utah in the 2016 Republican primary and in the EmpowerLA neighborhood elections got a taste of how convenient and secure it is to vote on the Internet, they will want to continue to have this option. Millennials, especially, are likely to start insisting on having the Internet voting option.[359]

Michael Shamos, Distinguished Career Professor in the School of Computer Science at Carnegie Mellon University, has conducted over 120 voting system examinations for seven states. He has testified about electronic voting before various committees of Congress and state legislatures. He told me,

Internet voting is absolutely inevitable and unstoppable. It will happen when the generation that was born with cellphones attached to their bodies comes into a position of power.[360]

Internet voting has the potential to change American democracy in a very positive way and lead to a stronger, representative democracy. Mobile voting could open the polls to many people who may feel disenfranchised today. The Digital Divide is a term that refers to the gap between demographics and regions which have access to modern information and communications technology and those that don't. Lower cost smartphones have reduced the divide. For example, The Wall Street Journal reported Latinos are adopting smartphones faster than other U.S. ethnic and racial groups.[361] Nielsen, the research firm, says 72% of Latinos over 18 own smartphones, nearly 10 percentage points higher than the national average.[362] Nearly half of Latinos, 49%, said they planned to upgrade their smartphones in the next six months.[363] I believe this segment of our population represents the trend toward acceptance of using a smartphone for many aspects of our lives.

The incredible power of smartphones in our pockets or purses will empower us to vote securely and privately, wherever we might be in the world. As voting becomes as simple as checking the weather or making an online purchase, voter participation will increase. Pilots such as Arizona, Utah, and West Virginia make this clear. I believe use of the mobile Internet will take participation to the next level. More importantly, increased voter participation can take democracy to the next level.

The majority of people I interviewed in my research for this book feel the American voting system has serious problems which are weakening our democracy. In both Republican and Democrat primary elections in 2016, Presidential candidates won the popular vote in a state but were denied the electoral votes because of state election rules. As of July 15, 2016, roughly a third of voters said that they are disappointed in the nominee of their party and were generally upset with how the political process is unfolding.[364] They feel the two party system is failing them.[365] Citizens feel the voting process is about money, not about them. Most estimates show the 2016 election will cost at least $3 billion. Many believe it will cost $5 billion, and some even put the number as high as $10 billion.[366]

The *Wall Street Journal* reported on July 15, 2016, "Despite pushback from health insurers, scrutiny by U.S. lawmakers, and the cries from citizens about rising prescription drug prices, pharmaceutical companies' power to raise prices is undeterred."[367] Special interest groups have a strong voice and they are heard. I believe citizens don't feel they have a voice. Strengthening of our democracy will take more than just additional, convenient elections every couple of years. It will require new methods of listening to citizens' voices and new ways for them to engage in public dialog. Internet voting will make such ideas possible.

The Voice of the People

Jerry Michalski, founder of REX, the Relationship Economy eXpedition, is a facilitator and explorer of the interactions between technology, society and business. He is a strong believer Internet voting can improve civic engagement. He said, "The system we have today is extremely far from a true democracy."[368] Democracy involves people getting involved in things they care about. Michalski says, "Voting every four years is dumb."[369] He would like to see ways developed in which people can work together to improve the system. His solution to the problem is to create a layer of discourse in which people can dig into an issue about which they care and engage with likeminded citizens. Michalski believes creating a platform about an issue and getting support for an online random sample of citizens' views could elevate the importance of the issue. Then, it could potentially get the attention of policymakers who can make changes.[370]

A traditional method of sampling what citizens think about issues or political choices is the poll. As Donald Trump's unexpected emergence as the nominee of the Republican Party and the U.K. vote to leave the European Union showed, polls can be way off the mark. Cliff Zukin is Professor of Public Policy and Political Science at Rutgers University and a Past President of the American Association for Public Opinion Research. He believes election polling is in near crisis. He said,

> Two trends are driving the increasing unreliability of election and other polling in the United States: the growth of cellphones and the decline in people willing to answer surveys. Coupled, they have made high-quality research much more expensive to do, so there is less of it. This has opened the door for less scientifically based, less well-tested techniques. In short, polls and pollsters are going to be less reliable. We may not even know when we're off base. What this means for 2016 is anybody's guess.[371]

Sampling The Voice of the People

With increased use of the Internet, new methods of sampling public opinion will be possible. One such method is known as random sample elections. The terminology is misleading, because random sample elections are not really elections. They are a technique of randomly selecting voters to get their opinion about an issue or a candidate proposal. The technique was developed by David Chaum, Ph.D., inventor of ecash and Digicash digital currencies, and numerous cryptographic protocols. Dr. Chaum devised a secure method of randomly selecting voters who would then receive a notice in the mail and be directed to a website featuring candidate debates and activist statements. Random choice voting is not a substitute for what we think of as voting today. It is way to strengthen our democracy by gaining statistically accurate input from citizens. I believe the public availability of such input would encourage more voter participation when it is time to select political leaders.

Dr. Chaum articulated his proposed sampling technique in a widely published white paper titled, "Random Choice Voting".[372] Chaum's research has shown only a small number of random voters are needed to accurately reflect the view of a large population from which the random voters were selected.[373] I believe the randomly sampled people would take more time to deliberate on issues privately at home. I think they would seek their own decision-making resources rather than being swayed by billions of dollars of advertising.

The white paper describes Chaum's ten "desirable characteristics" of random choice voting and compares it to a public election,

1) High voter turnout
2) Well informed voters
3) Effectiveness of results in shaping governance
4) Resistance to manipulation through advertising and electioneering
5) Indisputability of tally
6) Protection against voter corruption or coercion
7) Ensured access to vote casting
8) Resistance to voter fraud
9) Decisiveness
10) Low cost.[374]

Chaum said, "Current elections perform egregiously poorly against every single one of these ten positive attributes."[375] His white paper describes how random choice voting can address each of the ten attributes. A major benefit of the low cost characteristic and the requirement for only a small number of respondents needed is the sampling can be conducted frequently. Since citizens are chosen at random, an individual would not have to participate very often. There is no disenfranchisement as the purpose of random choice voting is to provide political leaders with valid input. It is not used to elect public officials but to gather opinions. The following is an example illustrating where a random sample on issues related to the cost of drugs and Medicare's restriction from negotiating the cost of drugs may have been valuable.

The *New York Times* reported a provision buried in the "fiscal cliff" bill passed by the U.S. Congress in January 2013 which gave Amgen, the world's largest biotechnology firm, a two year pass on Medicare's plan to regulate the cost of Sensipar, a drug used by kidney dialysis patients. The politicians behind the provision were Senators Max Baucus (D-Montana), and Orrin Hatch (R-Utah), both of whom had received campaign contributions from Amgen. The news about the provision's passing was so positive for Amgen the company communicated the coup to Wall Street analysts. The *Times* reported the provision is projected to cost Medicare up to $500 million over the two-year period.[376]

There are numerous issues for which the voice of the people could be heard more clearly using random sampling including: gun control, Medicare's ability to negotiate the price of drugs, term limits for Congress, declaring war, the federal budget deficit, and priorities for education, defense, public infrastructure, and energy. In today's system of representative democracy, citizens' points of view on major national issues are heard only every two years as we elect our representatives. After we elect them, we have no assurance they will hear or listen to our voices.

With the archaic system of voting we have today, it would not be practical to have frequent votes on major issues. If we had a pervasive election attitude, it would not be difficult to use Internet voting infrastructure to have national random samples of citizens' opinions on key issues on a regular basis or as needed. Informal polls using an online system could be used to determine if an issue has sufficient interest to justify a referendum, There are other methods which also could be used to strengthen our democracy such as the one in the next section.

Swiss Referenda

Switzerland has a system of democracy which gives citizens more power than in a representative democracy. Rather than have elected representatives vote on important issues, if at least 100,000 people support an issue, a vote goes to the entire 5.3 million registered voters. On June 5, 2016, five referenda were placed on the ballot. The one which got a lot of press coverage was called Basic Income Switzerland. The idea was to give all Swiss citizens a basic income, whether they are employed or not. The proposal would provide approximately $2,500 per month to all adults and $625 to all children. Supporters argued work was increasingly automated, fewer jobs were available for workers, and a significant amount of work takes place in homes and is not compensated. Opponents argued disconnecting the link between work done and money earned would be bad for society and encourage large numbers of people to immigrate to Switzerland. The measure was defeated 77% to 23%.[377]

The point about the Swiss vote is the people speak directly about an issue. In a representative democracy, we expect our elected representatives to vote on important issues on our behalf. The input the representatives receive is not by a vote of the people. In some cases, the input may come from special interest groups or even from a single company such as in the Amgen example. Sometimes a direct vote of the people can create a surprising outcome. On June 23, 2016, the people of Britain voted on the question of whether Britain should leave the European Union. After months of campaigning for or against leaving, 51.9 percent of voters, or 17.4 million people, voted to pull the U.K. out of the European Union.[378]

Ranked Choice Voting

William J. Kelleher, Ph.D., is CEO at The Internet Voting Research and Education Fund in Los Angeles. He wrote *Internet Voting Now: Here's How, Here's Why, So You Can Kiss Citizens United Goodbye.* Like Chaum, Michalski, and others, Dr. Kelleher believes Internet voting can lead to more civic engagement. He said,

> Lincoln's definition of democracy as A government of, by, and for the people implies citizen involvement – especially 'of' and 'by.' To me, more involvement means more opportunities to participate, and to make real decisions. The more real decisions people have the opportunity to make, the greater will be their sense of having real power, efficacy, and

ownership of government, and of responsibility for their political conditions. Internet voting has the potential to expand our conception of
citizenship way beyond what it means today, which is little more than the
obligation to vote a couple of times a year. [379]

Dr. Kelleher favors ranked choice voting, sometimes called instant run-off voting. Ranked choice voting is an alternative method of voting which Internet voting
could make possible. Ranked choice voting could be used when there are more
than two candidates. Instead of voting for one candidate, voters rank the candidates in order of preference, indicating first choice, second choice, third choice,
etc. for as many candidates as appear on a ballot. Kelleher says the ranked choice
voting method can,

> Avoid split votes and counter-majoritarian outcomes. Often, candidates
> can and do win election to offices like Governor despite being opposed
> by most voters. That's because when more than two candidates run, a
> majority of votes may be split among the two or more losing candidates.
> For example, in Maine, nine of the 11 gubernatorial elections between
> 1994 and 2014 were won with less than 50% of votes.[380]

Ranked choice voting eliminates the need for run-off elections which can be
expensive and delay results. Since 2000, more than ten cities have adopted the single
winner ranked choice voting method including Berkeley, Oakland, and San Leandro,
in California, Minneapolis and St. Paul, Minnesota, and Portland, Maine.[381] Ranked
choice voting is being used for the election of various public officials. For example,
Berkeley voters use ranked choice voting to elect the Mayor, Members of the City
Council, and the City Auditor. Oakland elects its Mayor, City Council members,
City Attorney, City Auditor, and School Directors using ranked choice voting. San
Leandro uses ranked choice voting to elect its Mayor and City Council members.

With ranked choice voting, if a candidate receives a majority of the first
choice votes cast for an office, that candidate will be elected. If no candidate
receives a majority of the first choice votes cast, the runoff process begins. The
candidate who received the fewest first-choice votes is eliminated. Next, each
vote cast for the losing candidate is transferred to the voter's next ranked choice
among the remaining candidates. The elimination process continues until a candidate receives a majority and is deemed the winner.

Ranked choice voting offers a number of advantages over the traditional voting process. There is no need for expensive runoff elections. In 2014, Alabama had a run-off election for several elected positions. It cost the state $3 million.[382] Ranked choice voting assures majority support. With traditional voting, candidates for Mayor and Governor can be elected even when most voters are opposed to them. With ranked choice voting, if no candidate wins more than half the vote from first choices, candidates finishing last are eliminated and the votes they received are reallocated until a winning candidate accumulates a majority compared to the other.

Another problem addressed by ranked choice voting is gerrymandering, a process whereby an entrenched minority can redefine congressional voting districts to bias how many representatives will be selected from each party in a state. Some have referred to the process as politicians picking their voters, instead of the other way around. Both Democrat and Republican politicians have used gerrymandering. A ranked choice voting process can ensure the majority of voters will always be able to elect a majority of seats, rather than the entrenched minority ensuring they stay in office.

Another advantage of ranked choice voting is it can discourage negative campaigning. This is not guaranteed, but in traditional voting elections, candidates sometimes benefit from "mudslinging". With ranked choice voting, candidates do best by connecting with as many voters as possible, including those voters who support an opponent. Rutgers University polled voters in seven cities with ranked choice voting in 2014. They discovered voters reported friendlier campaigns than during elections before ranked choice voting.[383]

Fair Vote

The strongest proponent of ranked choice voting is FairVote, a non-partisan, 501(c)(3) non-profit organization which seeks to make democracy fair, functional, and more representative. It conducts research and proposes common sense changes to strengthen our democracy. FairVote believes democracy is strongest when more voices are heard. Ranked choice voting, where more than two candidates compete without fear of splitting the vote, ensures all voices are heard and every vote counts in every election.[384]

FairVote believes ranked choice voting minimizes what they refer to as strategic voting. Voters should feel comfortable voting for candidates they support, not just against candidates they oppose. When there are only two candidates, voters may feel they need to vote for the lesser of two evils. By ranking multiple candidates, voters can feel they expressed their preferences without being influenced by mass media or social media about which of two candidates will win. The ranked choices allow people to think about all the candidates, not just or two.

Considering ranked choice voting in a Presidential context, the ballot might include Republicans Ted Cruz and Donald Trump, Democrats Hillary Clinton and Bernie Sanders, and Libertarian Gary Johnson. A more extensive ballot could have included the 17 candidates who were running during the early 2016 primary season. Rather than candidates spending enormous amounts of money on negative ads, they would have to focus on issues and building a positive, grassroots campaign for support from voters of any party. It would be very unlikely any of the expanded number of candidates would get a majority of the vote. The runoff process could reflect a better representation of what voters want than the traditional method of voting. Ranked choice voting can promote the representation of historically under-represented groups such as ethnic and racial minorities. A report co-authored by FairVote and the New America Foundation, a Washington, D.C. think tank, found racial minority populations prefer ranked choice voting, find it easy to use, and it would increase voter participation significantly.[385]

In theory, all cities could convert to ranked choice voting. In practice, it is not easy as evidenced by the fact only a handful have made the change. Cities without ranked choice voting cite two concerns. First, many cities do not have the proper equipment to perform the instant runoff. Existing voting machines are programmed to only count the number of votes for each candidate. Machines could be reprogrammed but that would require funding and lengthy approval processes. The concern about not having the funds to purchase new voting machines presents an excellent opportunity to move to Internet voting where ranked choice voting could be implemented on the existing voting server. A second concern is the confusion of voting for multiple candidates. As discussed in chapter 2, existing ballots are often complicated and confusing and result in lost votes. A webpage could be designed to make it easy to perform ranked choice voting. It could include a short video to show how it works.

Summary and Conclusions

Voter registration and election voting processes are complex topics. Because the Founding Fathers gave the States near autonomy to administer elections, it is difficult for changes to be made. In *Election Attitude*, I have examined some of the complexities and provided political leaders and election officials background material to help them as they consider alternatives to the aging voting infrastructure. The following summarizes the key issues and my recommendations.

1) Voter participation in America is low compared to other democracies. If the 2016 Presidential election attracts increased voters, the aging voting system may not be able to handle it. The system needs to upgrade using modern technology.

2) While America has been a leader in devising methods to use the Internet, it has not been a leader in developing modern voting solutions. Some states are encouraging voting by snail mail and increasing their dependence on the post office for timely ballot delivery. In the current election system, voters have no confirmation their mailed votes were counted.

3) The Internet, especially the mobile Internet, has permeated most aspects of our lives, except for voting. Physically going to a polling place is an old fashioned idea to millennials. They will begin to demand Internet voting.

4) A small group of anti-Internet voting activists who are opposed to Internet voting have dominated the dialog about the subject. They compare Internet voting to a perfect election system which is impossible to create rather than comparing it to the error prone, deficient and inefficient system being used now.

5) I advocate an election attitude which puts citizens first. Adopting an election attitude will lead to the development of systems which are easy to use and improve the registration process. When election officials and computer scientists adopt an election attitude, a system of Internet voting can be created which provides security, privacy, accuracy, verifiability, auditability, and reliability. As Internet pioneer Vint Cerf said, "We can do this."[386]

6) Achieving an election attitude requires pilots at all levels. A strong push should be made to resuscitate successful pilot projects and related research to establish Internet voting for the military. All military personnel have an ID card which can be the basis for a highly secure and accurate voting system. The military are providing us with protection. We should provide the military with the ability to vote securely and conveniently.

7) Pilot projects in Arizona, Utah, and West Virginia have demonstrated Internet voting is not only feasible, but also creates high voter satisfaction.

Voting jurisdictions should evaluate the success of these pilots and design additional ones.

8) States should evaluate successful Internet voting elections such as the City of Los Angeles Neighborhood Councils elections and write legislation leading to certification of standards to allow the use of Internet voting.

9) Election officials should challenge the naysayers who say "never" is too soon for Internet voting. They should challenge vendors to develop a combination of mobile Internet use, biometric identification of voters, and other advanced methods, such as blockchain technology, for secure recording and storage of votes.

10) Finding a cure for cancer is a more difficult challenge than developing a system for Internet voting, but political and medical leaders are approaching cancer research with vision and enthusiasm. The Moonshot 2020 cancer cure program has funding and leadership to solve a really challenging problem. Although the Federal Government cannot mandate how states run their elections, it could promote a strong vision for the advantages of a new election attitude, beginning with Internet voting for the military. The government leaders could provide states with encouragement to "Think Big", "Act Bold", "Start Simple", and "Iterate Fast".

On Tuesday, June 7, 2016, millions of Californians went to their local polling place. Many walked out disappointed. The *Los Angeles Times* reported it had nothing to do with candidates or politics. The voting problems had to do with broken vote counting machines, moved polling sites, or inaccurate voting registers. Some voters possibly walked out because the lines were too long and they couldn't wait. Others filled out a paper provisional ballot, inserted it into an envelope, but with no assurance it would get delivered or would be counted properly.

Melissa Batchelor Warnke, author of the *Times* story said,

Each person walking around California with a smartphone carries a ridiculous amount of computing power on their person. They have the ability to play games with strangers on another continent, comment on the baby photos of someone they haven't seen in 10 years or take slow-motion videos. We are living in a time of rapid technological innovation, so we expect things to work. Imagine walking into a polling station and realizing that they don't have your name on an official list printed in an official binder -- even though you registered -- because another piece of paper was misplaced somewhere along the way from the county registrar's office. So now you've got to write your vote on this piece of paper that won't be counted by a human until after the initial results are announced.[387]

California has seen 2016 voter registration reach a record high, including increases in numbers of young people and non-native English speakers. The increase is good news. The bad news is the antiquated and failing voting system remains. Warnke expressed my beliefs with the following election attitude which exudes a positive and constructive suggestion,

Yes, California -- the state that birthed the self-driving car and the polygraph machine and the space shuttle Endeavor -- is having a really hard time tracking the little pieces of paper they send in the mail from one location to another. That's making its systems glitchy when volunteers at the polls try to figure out who you are and what kind of ballot you should receive. Perhaps in addition to creating apps to make our lives more comfortable, Silicon Valley could donate a bit of its attention to revamping California's voting system.[388]

Problems with the voting process are not limited to California. Election precincts across the country are facing many of the same problems. In addition to a lack of adequate funding for new equipment, election officials need to learn and implement the new voting methods which consumers are demanding. I believe an increasing number of voters will start questioning why we can't vote from our smartphones over the Internet.

Computer scientists across the country have accomplished extraordinary developments in cloud computing, analytics for big data, the Internet of Things, artificial intelligence, and an inter-planetary Internet. All of these areas faced skeptics and critics who said, "It couldn't be done". I believe working with election officials, voting machine vendors, computer scientists, and software engineers we can solve the challenges and complexities of Internet voting. As a result, Americans could be proud of a stronger democracy with the highest voter participation in the world.

West Virginia Secretary of State, Natalie Tennant, summed up an election attitude very well,

> Instead of continuing to focus on the shortcomings of Internet voting, opponents could help strengthen it. Computer experts could lend their skills to developing encryption software that guarantees that each ballot is securely transmitted. Election officials could help voters better understand how the process works. Internet voting should be a safe, secure, accessible option for voters. It is time that we, as a society, agree that our voting is far too sacred to compromise — and that at some point in time this sacred right and accessible technology must intersect. I believe the time to explore that is now.[389]

Join me in working toward a new election attitude which leads to a stronger democracy.

Acknowledgements

There are a number of people I would like to thank for helping me with *Election Attitude*. First and foremost is Tom Lutz. Writing a book about this important topic was his idea. Second is Kathleen Imhoff. Her editing skills are unparalleled. Every day over a period of months, Kathleen offered countless suggestions which crystallized the story I want to tell. I would like to thank Bill Kelleher. His book inspired me to do the research for *Election Attitude*. I would like to offer a special thanks to Conny McCormack and Ted Selker. Their intimate knowledge of voting processes and broad perspective of the voting industry contributed greatly to *Election Attitude*.

I am grateful for the time and interest of the following who contributed their ideas, quotations, or comments on early drafts: Ben Adida, Michael Alvarez, Steve Ansolabehere, Paul Babic, Josh Benaloh, Gene Bolton, Stephen Box, Chuck Callan, Vint Cerf, David Chaum, Cindy Cohn, Lori Steele Contorer, Jerry Cuomo, David Dill, Adam Ernest, Dave Farber, Stu Feldman, Bob Greenberg, Ron Gruner, Paul Lux, Jerry Michalski, Greg Miller, Harris Miller, Joe Mohen, Regina Ofiero, Aaron Patrick, Joanne Patrick, Tracy Patrick-Panchelli, Bill Raduchel, Pamela Smith, Nick Spanos, Charles Stewart, Mike Summers, Briana Wilson, and John Wolpert.

Appendices

Appendix A: Votes Cast in OECD Countries

Rank	Country (Year)	% of voting age population	% of registered voters
1	Belgium (2014)*	87.20%	89.40%
2	Turkey (2011)*	86.40%	87.20%
3	Sweden (2014)	82.60%	85.80%
4	Denmark (2011)	81.80%	87.70%
5	Australia (2013)*	80.50%	93.20%
6	South Korea (2012)	80.40%	75.80%
7	Iceland (2013)	80.00%	81.40%
8	Norway (2013)	77.90%	78.20%
9	Israel (2015)	76.10%	72.30%
10	New Zealand (2014)	73.20%	77.90%
11	Finland (2015)	73.10%	66.90%
12	Greece (2015)*	71.90%	63.60%
13	France (2012)	71.20%	80.40%
14	Netherlands (2012)	71.00%	74.60%
15	Austria (2013)	69.30%	74.90%
16	Italy (2013)	68.50%	75.20%
17	Germany (2013)	66.00%	71.50%

Source: Pew Research Center.[390] An * signifies countries where voting is mandatory.

Appendix A (*continued*)

Rank	Country (Year)	% of voting age population	% of registered voters
18	Mexico (2012)*	64.60%	63.10%
19	Ireland (2011)	63.80%	69.90%
20	Hungary (2014)	63.40%	61.80%
21	Spain (2011)	63.30%	68.90%
22	U.K. (2010)	61.10%	65.80%
23	Czech Republic (2013)	60.00%	59.50%
24	Slovakia (2012)	57.80%	59.10%
25	Portugal (2011)	56.60%	58.90%
26	Luxembourg (2013)*	55.10%	91.10%
27	Estonia (2015)	54.70%	64.20%
28	Poland (2010)	54.50%	55.30%
29	Canada (2011)	54.20%	61.10%
30	Slovenia (2014)	54.10%	51.70%
31	United States (2012)	53.60%	84.30%
32	Japan (2014)	52.00%	52.70%
33	Chile (2013)	45.70%	42.00%
34	Switzerland (2011)	40.00%	49.10%

Source: Pew Resear ch Center.[391] An * signifies countries where voting is mandatory.

About the Author

D r. John R. Patrick is President of Attitude LLC and former Vice President of Internet Technology at IBM, where he worked for thirty-five years. John was a founding member of the World Wide Web Consortium at MIT in 1994, a founding member and past chairman of the Global Internet Project, a member of the Internet Society and the American College of Healthcare Executives, a senior member of the Association for Computing Machinery, and a Fellow of the Institute of Electrical and Electronics Engineers. John is a board member at Keeeb Inc. and OCLC, and is a member of the Western Connecticut Health Network Biomedical Research Institute Advisory Council. John holds a Doctor of Health Administration (DHA) from University of Phoenix, an MS in Management from the University of South Florida, an LLB in Law from LaSalle Extension University, and a BS in Electrical Engineering from Lehigh University. He is the author of Health Attitude and Net Attitude. John lives in Danbury, CT and Palm Coast, FL with his wife Joanne. His website is at attitudellc.org and you can contact him at john@attitudellc.org or on Twitter @johnrpatrick.

Notes

1   "Quarterly Retail E-Commerce Sales 3rd Quarter 2015," *U.S. Census Bureau News. U.S. Department of Commerce* (2015), https://www.census.gov/retail/mrts/www/data/pdf/ec_current.pdf.

2   Ibid.

3   "U.S. Voter Turnout Trails Most Developed Countries," *Pew Research Center* (2015), http://www.pewresearch.org/fact-tank/2015/05/06/u-s-voter-turnout-trails-most-developed-countries/.

4   "Gun Control," *Pew Research Center* (2016), http://www.pewresearch.org/topics/gun-control/.

5   "Guns," *PollingReport.com* (2016), http://www.pollingreport.com/guns.htm.

6   "Senate Vote 97 - Defeats Manchin-Toomey Background Checks Proposal," *The New York Times* (2013), http://politics.nytimes.com/congress/votes/113/senate/1/97.

7   Andrew Egger, "See How Your Senators Voted on 4 Gun Control Amendments," *The Daily Signal* (2016), http://dailysignal.com/2016/06/21/see-how-your-senators-voted-on-4-gun-control-amendments/.

8   "Tesla Model S Rated #1 in Customer Satisfaction," *Inside EVs*, http://insideevs.com/consumer-reports-tesla-model-s-rated-1-in-customer-satisfaction/.

9   Eva GrantSimran Khosla, "Here's Everywhere Uber Is Banned around the World," *Business Insider* (2015), http://www.businessinsider.com/heres-everywhere-uber-is-banned-around-the-world-2015-4.

10   "The Gettysburg Address," *Abraham Lincoln Online* (2016), http://www.abrahamlincolnonline.org/lincoln/speeches/gettysburg.htm.

11   "American Political Attitudes and Participation," *American Government* (2014), http://www.ushistory.org/gov/index.asp.

12   "1992 Census of Governments," *United States Census Bureau* (1992), http://www.census.gov/prod/2/gov/gc/gc92_1_2.pdf.

13   "California 2016 Ballot Propositions," *BallotPedia* (2016), https://ballotpedia.org/California_2016_ballot_propositions.

14   Ibid.

15   Ibid.

16   "About State Legislatures," *National Conference of State Legislatures* (2016), http://www.ncsl.org/research/about-state-legislatures.aspx.

17   "Local Governments by Type and State: 2012 - United States," *United States Census Bureau* (2012), http://factfinder.census.gov/faces/tableservices/jsf/pages/productview.xhtml?src=bkmk.

18   "1992 Census of Governments".

19   "Voting and Registration in the Election of November 2012," *United States Census Bureau* (2015), https://www.census.gov/hhes/www/socdemo/voting/publications/p20/2012/tables.html.

20 "Felony Disenfranchisement," *The Sentencing Project* (2016), http://www.sentencingproject.org/template/page.cfm?id=133.

21 Ibid.

22 J. Chung, "Felony Disenfranchisement: A Primer," ibid., http://sentencingproject.org/doc/publications/fd_Felony%20Disenfranchisement%20Primer.pdf.

23 "Felony Disenfranchisement," ibid., http://www.sentencingproject.org/template/page.cfm?id=133.

24 "Felony Disenfranchisement: A Primer," ibid., http://sentencingproject.org/doc/publications/fd_Felony%20Disenfranchisement%20Primer.pdf.

25 SHERYL GAY STOLBERG and ERIK ECKHOLM, "Virginia Governor Restores Voting Rights to Felons," *The New York Times* (2016), http://www.nytimes.com/2016/04/23/us/governor-terry-mcauliffe-virginia-voting-rights-convicted-felons.html.

26 "U.S. Voter Turnout Trails Most Developed Countries".

27 Ibid.

28 Ibid.

29 "Voting and Registration in the Election of November 2012".

30 "History for the Mind... And Heart," *UShistory.org* (2016), UShistory.org.

31 "American Political Attitudes and Participation".

32 "Register to Vote," *USA.gov* (2016), https://www.usa.gov/register-to-vote#item-212447.

33 "Voter Id Requirements," *North Dakota State Government* (2016), https://vip.sos.nd.gov/PortalListDetails.aspx?ptlhPKID=103&ptlPKID=7.

34   "Welcome to the Illinois Online Voter Registration Application Website," *Illinois Online Voter Registration Application: State Board of Elections* (2016), https://ova.elections.il.gov.

35   Laurie Meisler Chloe Whiteaker, Yvette Romero, "States That Make Voting Super Simple–or Stupidly Hard," (2014), http://www.bloomberg.com/politics/graphics/2014-states-where-voting-is-easiest/.

36   "Public Policy in Wisconsin," *BallotPedia* (2016), https://ballotpedia.org/Voting_in_Wisconsin.

37   "Voting Laws Roundup 2014," *Brennan Center for Justice* (2014), http://www.brennancenter.org/analysis/voting-laws-roundup-2014.

38   Ibid.

39   Ibid.

40   Adam Liptak, "Supreme Court Invalidates Key Part of Voting Rights Act," *The New York Times* (2013), http://www.nytimes.com/2013/06/26/us/supreme-court-ruling.html.

41   "Bipartisan Bill Introduced: Congress Must Restore Voting Rights Act," *Brennan Center for Justice* (2015), https://www.brennancenter.org/press-release/bipartisan-bill-introduced-congress-must-restore-voting-rights-act.

42   Richard Wolf, "Supreme Court Won't Block Texas Photo Id Law — Yet," *USA Today* (2016), http://www.usatoday.com/story/news/politics/2016/04/29/supreme-court-texas-voting-photo-id/83075938/.

43   "Voting Laws Roundup 2014".

44   "Bipartisan Bill Introduced: Congress Must Restore Voting Rights Act".

45   "H.R. 3899 (113th): Voting Rights Amendment Act of 2014," *govtrack.us* (2015), https://www.govtrack.us/congress/bills/113/hr3899.

46 Tom Huskerson, "A Brief History of Voter Registration in the United States," *Independent Voter Project* (2014), A Brief History of Voter Registration in the United States.

47 Ibid.

48 Ibid.

49 "The American Voting Experience: Report and Recommendations of the Presidential Commission on Election Administration," *Presidential Commission on Election Administration* (2014), https://www.supportthev-oter.gov/files/2014/01/Amer-Voting-Exper-final-draft-01-09-14-508.pdf.

50 Barry C. Burden and Jacob R. Neiheisel, "Election Administration and the Pure Effect of Voter Registration on Turnout," *Political Research Quarterly 66*, no. 1 (2013).

51 Rene R. Rocha and Tetsuya Matsubayashi, "The Politics of Race and Voter Id Laws in the States: The Return of Jim Crow?," ibid.67, no. 3 (2014).

52 "National Voter Registration Day Is Marked by over 2,100 Community Partnerships and Hundreds of Voter Registration Events across the Country," *National Voter Registration Day* (2015), http://nationalvoterregistrationday. org/about/2015-press-release/.

53 Ibid.

54 "States Make Advances in Voter Registration," *The Pew Charitable Trusts* (2016), http://www.pewtrusts.org/en/research-and-analysis/analysis/2016/02/03/ states-make-advances-in-voter-registration.

55 Ibid.

56 Chloe Whiteaker, "States That Make Voting Super Simple–or Stupidly Hard".

57 "American Political Attitudes and Participation".

58   Adam Liptak, "As Voting by Mail Rises, So Do Problems with Ballots,"
      The New York Times (2012), https://www.bostonglobe.com/news/na-
      tion/2012/10/06/voting-mail-leads-fraud-ignored-ballots/ivnPG2sgLnoD-
      6IzBaY0UDK/story.html.

59   "American Political Attitudes and Participation".

60   Ibid.

61   Ted Selker, telephone and email conversations with author, July 14, 2016.

62   Arend Lijphart, "Unequal Participation: Democracy's Unresolved Dilemma,"
      The American Political Science Review (1997), http://www.people.fas.harvard.
      edu/~iversen/PDFfiles/Lijphart1997.pdf.

63   "Why Do Americans Vote on Tuesdays?," *Why Tuesday?* (2014), http://www.
      whytuesday.org/faq/.

64   Ibid.

65   Scott Keyes, "Seven Voting Reforms Other Countries Have Used to Boost
      Their Turnout Rate," *ThinkProgress* (2013), http://thinkprogress.org/
      justice/2013/05/15/2000621/international-voting-reforms/.

66   "The National Voter Registration Act of 1993 (Nvra)," *United States
      Department of Justice* (2015), http://www.justice.gov/crt/national-voter-
      registration-act-1993-nvra.

67   1996, "Motor Voter or Motivated Voter?," *The American Prospect* (Marshall
      Ganz), http://prospect.org/article/motor-voter-or-motivated-voter.

68   Ibid.

69   Ibid.

70   "American Political Attitudes and Participation".

71   "Automatic Voter Registration," *Brennan Center for Justice* (2016), https://www.brennancenter.org/analysis/automatic-voter-registration.

72   EditorialBoard, "The Worst Voter Turnout in 72 Years," *The New York Times* (2014), http://www.nytimes.com/2014/11/12/opinion/the-worst-voter-turnout-in-72-years.html.

73   Drew Desilver, "So Far, Turnout in This Year's Primaries Rivals 2008 Record," *FactTank* (2016), http://www.pewresearch.org/fact-tank/2016/03/08/so-far-turnout-in-this-years-primaries-rivals-2008-record/.

74   "Voting Systems & Use: 1980-2012," *ProCon.org* (2016), http://votingmachines.procon.org/view.resource.php?resourceID=000274#mechanical_lever.

75   Ibid.

76   John Sheesley, "Y2k: The New Year's Disaster That Never Happened," *TechRepublic* (2009), http://www.techrepublic.com/blog/classics-rock/y2k-the-new-years-disaster-that-never-happened/.

77   Ted Selker, "Fixing the Vote: Electronic Voting Machines Promise to Make Fixing Elections More Accurate Than Ever before, but Only If Certain Problems—with the Machines and the Wider Electoral Process—Are Rectified," *Scientific American* (2004), http://vote.caltech.edu/sites/default/files/fixing_the_vote.pdf.

78   "Glossary of Terms Used by Palm Beach County, Florida, Canvassing Board," *nightscribe.com* (2016), http://www.nightscribe.com/politics/chadology.htm.

79   BSuddreth, "Summary of the 2000 Presidential Election," *2000 Presidential Election: Information and Media Resources* (2012), http://www.2000presidentialelection.com/summary-of-the-2000-presidential-election/.

80   Selker, "Fixing the Vote: Electronic Voting Machines Promise to Make Fixing Elections More Accurate Than Ever before, but Only If Certain

Problems—with the Machines and the Wider Electoral Process—Are Rectified".

81   Ibid.

82   Ibid.

83   "Election of 2000: Year of the Hanging Chad," *united States History* (2013), http://www.u-s-history.com/pages/h916.html.

84   "Help America Vote Act," *United States Election Assistance Commission* (2015), http://www.eac.gov/about_the_eac/help_america_vote_act.aspx.

85   "Voting Systems & Use: 1980-2012".

86   Ibid.

87   "The 2014 Eac Election Administration and Voting Survey Comprehensive Report," *U.S. Election Assistance Commission* (2015), http://www.eac.gov/assets/1/Page/2014_EAC_EAVS_Comprehensive_Report_508_Compliant.pdf.

88   Ibid.

89   "The American Voting Experience: Report and Recommendations of the Presidential Commission on Election Administration".

90   Ibid.

91   Ibid.

92   Lawrence Norden and Christopher Famighetti, "America's Voting Machines at Risk," (2015), https://www.brennancenter.org/sites/default/files/publications/Americas_Voting_Machines_At_Risk.pdf.

93 "The 2014 Eac Election Administration and Voting Survey Comprehensive Report".

94 "Rep. Johnson Introduces Bill to Upgrade Aging, Outdated Voting Machines," *U.S. House of Representatives Media Center* (2016), http://hankjohnson.house.gov/press-release/rep-johnson-introduces-bill-upgrade-aging-outdated-voting-machines.

95 Ibid.

96 Ari Berman, "There Were 5-Hour Lines to Vote in Arizona Because the Supreme Court Gutted the Voting Rights Act," *The Nation* (2016), http://www.thenation.com/article/there-were-five-hour-lines-to-vote-in-arizona-because-the-supreme-court-gutted-the-voting-rights-act/.

97 Ibid.

98 Ibid.

99 Matt O'Brien, "Rhode Island Says It Can Handle Primary with Fewer Polling Places," *Providence Journal* (2016), http://www.providencejournal.com/article/20160421/NEWS/160429785.

100 Ibid.

101 Josh Dawsey, "New York City Board of Elections Official Suspended," *The Wall Street Journal* (2016), http://www.wsj.com/articles/new-york-city-board-of-elections-official-suspended-1461276473.

102 Ibid.

103 Ibid.

104 Harris Miller, telephone conversation with author, June 28, 2016.

105 "Florida Election Problems: Some Polling Locations Ran out of Ballots or Had Wrong Ones," *News13* (2016), http://www.mynews13.com/content/news/cfnews13/news/article.html/content/news/articles/cfn/2016/3/15/voters_met_with_tech.html.

106 Ibid.

107 Paul S. Herrnson, Richard G. Niemi, and Michael J. Hanmer, *Voting Technology: The Not-So-Simple Act of Casting a Ballot* (Washington, US: Brookings Institution Press, 2009).

108 Marvin Joseph, "The Dismal State of America's Decade-Old Voting Machines," *Wired* (2015), https://www.wired.com/2015/09/dismal-state-americas-decade-old-voting-machines/.

109 Ibid.

110 Ibid.

111 Douglas W. Jones, "On Optical Mark-Sense Scanning," *University of Iowa* (2010), http://homepage.cs.uiowa.edu/~jones/voting/OpticalMarkSenseScanning.pdf.

112 Douglas Jones and B. Simons, *Broken Ballots : Will Your Vote Count?* (Stanford, Calif.: CSLI Publications, 2012).

113 Ibid.

114 Paul Taylor, "Why Hasn't Voting by Mail Spread?," *Governing* (2011), http://www.governing.com/columns/dispatch/Why-Hasnt-Voting-by-Mail-Spread.html.

115 "Absentee and Early Voting," *National Conference of State Legislatures* (2016), http://www.ncsl.org/research/elections-and-campaigns/absentee-and-early-voting.aspx.

116 "Voting by Mail," *The New York Times* (2012), http://www.nytimes.com/interactive/2012/10/07/us/voting-by-mail.html?_r=0.

117 Ibid.

118 Ibid.

119 Ibid.

120 Ibid.

121 "Vote by Mail," *FairVote* (2016), http://archive.fairvote.org/turnout/mail.htm.

122 "Election Administration and Voting Survey," *United States Election Assistance Commission* (2014), http://www.eac.gov/research/election_administration_and_voting_survey.aspx.

123 "The 2014 Eac Election Administration and Voting Survey Comprehensive Report".

124 Ted Selker.

125 "Uniformed and Overseas Citizens Absentee Voting Act (Uocava)," *Federal Voting Assistance Program. U.S. Department of Defense* (2007), http://web.archive.org/web/20080717085438/http://www.fvap.gov/laws/uocavalaw.html.

126 "The 2014 Eac Election Administration and Voting Survey Comprehensive Report".

127 "Military Voting Update: A Bleak Picture in 2012," *Military Voter Protection Project* (2012), http://mvpproject.org/wp-content/uploads/2012/08/Bleak-Picture-for-Military-Voters.pdf.

128 William J. Kelleher, *Internet Voting Now: Here's How, Here's Why, So You Can Kiss Citizens United Goodbye!* (Los Angeles, CA: Internet Voting Research and Education Fund, 2011).

129 ""No Time to Vote" for Many Military Personnel Overseas," *The Pew Charitable Trusts* (2009), http://www.pewtrusts.org/en/about/news-room/press-releases/2009/01/06/no-time-to-vote-for-many-military-personnel-overseas-pew-study-finds.

130 *Internet Voting Now: Here's How, Here's Why, So You Can Kiss Citizens United Goodbye!*

131 "Internet Voting: The Great Security Scare," *FCC.gov* (2010), http://apps.fcc.gov/ecfs/document/view;jsessionid=xjrGSnZJC1y11n1JFLzGvQNpQDGhLl q2Jn5FKmvJdJ8lFb28yBtd!608620108!-739454830?id=7020355817.

132 Thad E. Hall and R. Michael Alvarez, "Voting Online around the World," *Caltech/MIT Voting Technology Project* (2008), http://vote.caltech.edu/sites/default/files/Hall%20Alvarez%20VIA3.pdf.

133 David Jefferson et al., "A Security Analysis of the Secure Electronic Registration and Voting Experiment (Serve)," *Server Security Report* (2004), http://www.servesecurityreport.org.

134 Ibid.

135 Kelleher, "Internet Voting: The Great Security Scare".

136 Ibid.

137 "Military Voting Update: A Bleak Picture in 2012".

138 Ibid.

139 "Internet Voting: The Great Security Scare".

140 "Review of Fvap's Work Related to Remote Electronic Voting for the Uocava Population," *Federal Voting Assistance Program* (2015), https://www.fvap.gov/uploads/FVAP/Reports/FVAP_EVDP_20151229_final.pdf.

141 R. Michael Alvarez and Thad E. Hall, "Electronic Elections the Perils and Promises of Digital Democracy," (2008).

142 Dave Farber, telephone conversation with author, May 5, 2016.

143 "Electronic Elections the Perils and Promises of Digital Democracy."

144 Charles Stewart III, "Losing Votes by Mail," *Support the Voter* (2006), https://www.supportthevoter.gov/files/2013/08/Losing-Votes-by-Mail.pdf.

145 Ibid.

146 Thomas W. Hazlett, Sarah Oh, and Drew Clark, "The Overly Active Corpse of Red Lion," *Northwestern Journal of Technology & Intellectual Property* (2010), http://scholarlycommons.law.northwestern.edu/njtip/.

147 Steven Rosenfeld, "Http://Scholarlycommons.Law.Northwestern.Edu/Njtip/," *Alternet* (2016), http://www.alternet.org/election-2016/accusations-fraud-and-theft-fly-after-iowa-vote-heres-lowdown.

148 Justin Levitt, "The Truth About Voter Fraud," *Brennan Center for Justice* (2007), https://www.brennancenter.org/publication/truth-about-voter-fraud.

149 Ibid.

150 Tracy Campbell, *Deliver the Vote : A History of Election Fraud, an American Political Tradition, 1742-2004* (New York: Carroll & Graf, 2005).

151 Kevin Pallister, "Interesting Material, Mediocre Execution," *Amazon* (2012), http://www.amazon.com/review/R1LVEF09AU2FW1/ref=cm_cr_dp_title?ie=UTF8&ASIN=0786718439&channel=detail-glance&nodeID=283155&store=books.

152   Lorraine Carol Minnite, *The Myth of Voter Fraud* (Ithaca [N.Y.]: Cornell University Press, 2010).

153   Ben Pryor, "Why It's Time to End in-Person Voting for Good," *New Republic* (2016), https://newrepublic.com/article/130494/its-time-end-in-person-voting-good.

154   "Selker Honored for Aiding Voting for Disabled," *MIT News* (2006), http://news.mit.edu/2006/voting.

155   "Stihl Products," *Stihl* (2016), http://www.stihlusa.com/products/.

156   Jillian D'Onfro, "14 Quirky Things You Didn't Know About Amazon," *Business Insider* (2014), http://www.businessinsider.com/amazon-jeff-bezos-facts-story-history-2014-5.

157   "Amazon.Com," *Wikipedia* (2016), https://en.wikipedia.org/wiki/Amazon.com.

158   John R. Patrick, *Net Attitude : What It Is, How to Get It, and Why You Need It More Than Ever* (Palm Coast, FL: Attitude LLC, 2016).

159   "How Many Products Does Amazon Sell?," *Exportx* (2016), https://export-x.com/2015/12/11/how-many-products-does-amazon-sell-2015/.

160   Paul Grey, ibid., (2013), https://export-x.com/2013/12/15/many-products-amazon-sell/.

161   "Amazon.Com, Inc. (Amzn)," *Yahoo! Finance* (2016), http://finance.yahoo.com/q?s=AMZN.

162   Ted Selker.

163   "Quarterly Retail E-Commerce Sales 3rd Quarter 2015".

164   "Irs E-File: A History," *IRS* (2011), https://www.irs.gov/uac/IRS-E-File:-A-History.

165 "U.S. Taxpayers Efiled More Than 128 Million Returns in 2015," *efile.com* (2015), http://www.efile.com/efile-tax-return-direct-deposit-statistics/.

166 "E-File Overview," *IRS* (2016), https://www.irs.gov/Tax-Professionals/e-File-Providers-&-Partners/e-file-Overview.

167 "Irs Statement on E-Filing Pin," *IRS* (2016), https://www.irs.gov/uac/Newsroom/IRS-Statement-on-Efiling-PIN.

168 "Improved Technology and Better in-Person Interactions with Millennials Drive Historic Performance Improvement among Nation's Largest Retail Banks," *J.D. Power* (2016), http://www.jdpower.com/press-releases/2016-us-retail-banking-satisfaction-study.

169 Ibid.

170 Marcia Kaplan, "B2b Ecommerce Growing; Becoming More Like B2c," *PracticalEcommerce* (2015), http://www.practicalecommerce.com/articles/85970-B2B-Ecommerce-Growing-Becoming-More-Like-B2C.

171 Ibid.

172 Barry Ritholtz, "Where Have All the Public Companies Gone?," *BloombergView* (2015), https://www.bloomberg.com/view/articles/2015-06-24/where-have-all-the-publicly-traded-companies-gone-.

173 "Broadridge Insights," *Broadridge* (2015), http://www.broadridge.com/broadridge-insights/Key-Statistics-and-Performance-Ratings-for-the-Proxy-Season.html.

174 Ibid.

175 "World Payments Report 2015," *Word Payments Report* (2015), https://www.worldpaymentsreport.com.

176 Matt Phillips, "The Spectacular Decline of Checks," *The Atlantic* (2014), http://www.theatlantic.com/business/archive/2014/06/the-rise-and-fall-of-checks/372217/.

177 Lance Ulanoff, "Just How Big Is the Apple Pay Mobile Payment Pie?," *Mashable* (2015), http://mashable.com/2015/01/29/apple-pay-mobile-payment-pie/#2R5ARcM24ZqY.

178 "World Payments Report 2015".

179 Ibid.

180 Alex Konrad, "Spurning Ipo, Surveymonkey Now Allows You to Compare Data with Rivals," (2015), http://www.forbes.com/sites/alexkonrad/2015/04/02/surveymonkey-now-allows-you-to-compare-data-with-rivals-for-a-price/#64727653190e.

181 Ibid.

182 Sherree Geyer, "Patient Portals More Useful Than Many Realize," *Healthcare IT News* (2015), http://www.healthcareitnews.com/news/patient-portals-more-useful-many-realize.

183 Mary Rechtoris, "5 Trends Sweeping Healthcare," *Becker's ASCReview* (2016), http://www.beckersasc.com/asc-turnarounds-ideas-to-improve-performance/5-trends-sweeping-healthcare.html.

184 "Is Internet Security Getting Better or Worse?," *Zombie Code Kill* (2015), https://zombiecodekill.com/2015/11/02/is-internet-security-getting-better-or-worse/.

185 "Welcome to Estonia," *Estonia.eu* (2016), http://estonia.eu/index.html.

186 "Internet Voting in Estonia," *Varabiigi Valimiskomisjon* (2016), http://vvk.ee/voting-methods-in-estonia/.

187 "Statistics About Internet Voting in Estonia," *Varabiigi Valimiskomisjon* (2016), http://vvk.ee/voting-methods-in-estonia/engindex/statistics.

188 Ibid.

189 "Internet Voting in Estonia".

190 Charles Arthur, "Estonian E-Voting Shouldn't Be Used in European Elections, Say Security Experts," *theguardian* (2014), https://www.theguardian.com/technology/2014/may/12/estonian-e-voting-security-warning-european-elections-research.

191 Ibid.

192 UMichSecurityLab, "Security Analysis of the Estonian E-Voting System," *Independent Report on E-voting in Estonia* (2014), https://estoniaevoting.org.

193 Ibid.

194 Anto Veldre, "E-Voting Is (Too) Secure," *Republic of Estonia Information System Authority* (2014), https://www.ria.ee/en/e-voting-is-too-secure.html.

195 Ibid.

196 Anto Veldre, email communication with author, April 30, 2016.

197 Ibid.

198 "E-Voting Is (Too) Secure".

199 "E-Voting Concept Security: Analysis and Measures," *National Electoral Committee* (2010), http://www.vvk.ee/public/dok/E-voting_concept_security_analysis_and_measures_2010.pdf.

200 "E-Voting Is (Too) Secure".

201 "President Toomas Hendrik Ilves Speech at Icegov 2011 Conference," *e-estonia. com* (2011), https://e-estonia.com/president-toomas-hendrik-ilves-speech-icegov-2011-conference/.

202 "E-Voting Is (Too) Secure".

203 "Internet Voting Outside the United States," *Verified Voting* (2014), https://www.verifiedvoting.org/internet-voting-outside-the-united-states/.

204 "E-Voting," *ch.ch* (2016), https://www.ch.ch/en/online-voting/.

205 Conny B. McCormack, "Democracy Rebooted: The Future of Technology in Elections," *Atlantic Council* (2016), http://publications.atlanticcouncil.org/election-tech/assets/report.pdf.

206 Daniel Rubin, "The Security of Remote Online Voting" (University of Virginia, 2001).

207 "A Survey of Internet Voting," *U.S. Election Assistance Commission* (2011), http://www.eac.gov/assets/1/Documents/SIV-FINAL.pdf.

208 "The Security of Remote Online Voting."

209 "Judge Lets Internet Primary in Arizona Proceed," *The New York Times* (2000), http://www.nytimes.com/2000/03/01/technology/01vote.html.

210 Doug Bernard, "Internet Voting Unlikely to Replace Paper Ballots in US," *Voice of America* (2016), http://www.voanews.com/content/internet-voting-unlikely-replace-paper-ballots-in-us/3259088.html.

211 Berman, "There Were 5-Hour Lines to Vote in Arizona Because the Supreme Court Gutted the Voting Rights Act".

212 Rubin, "The Security of Remote Online Voting."

213 Paul Lux, telephone conversation with author, July 7, 2016.

214 Ibid.

215 Ibid.

216 Ibid.

217 "Michigan Dems Vote Online," *Wired* (2004), http://www.wired.com/2004/02/michigan-dems-vote-online/.

218 Ibid.

219 "Just over 46,000 Vote Online in Michigan Democratic Caucuses," *USA Today: Campaign 2004* (2004), http://usatoday30.usatoday.com/news/politicselections/nation/president/2004-02-07-internet-voting_x.htm.

220 Ibid.

221 Ibid.

222 Alicia Kolar Prevost and Brian F. Schaffner, "Digital Divide or Just Another Absentee Ballot?: Evaluating Internet Voting in the 2004 Michigan Democratic Primary," *American Politics Research*, no. 36 (2008).

223 "A Survey of Internet Voting".

224 Natalie E. Tennant, "Making the Case for Online Voting," *government technology* (2012), http://www.govtech.com/e-government/Making-the-Case-for-Online-Voting.html.

225 Ibid.

226 Ibid.

227 "Americans Elect 2012," *americanselect.org* (2012), http://www.americanselect.org.

228 Lois Kazakoff, "Draft Your Nominee for President," *SFGate Opinion Shop* (2012), http://blog.sfgate.com/opinionshop/2012/02/02/draft-your-nominee-for-president/.

229 Ruth Marcus, "Americans Elect: A Wild Card for the Internet Age," *The Washington Post* (2011), https://www.washingtonpost.com/opinions/americans-elect-a-wild-card-for-the-internet-age/2011/12/27/gIQAPYlILP_story.html.

230 Amy Bingham, "Americans Elect' Ends Online Primary after No Candidates Qualify to Run," *abc News* (2012), http://abcnews.go.com/blogs/politics/2012/05/americans-elect-ends-online-primary-after-no-candidates-qualify-to-run/.

231 David Weigel, "Nobody for President: The Inevitable, Glorious, $35 Million Failure of Americans Elect," *Slate Politics* (2012), http://www.slate.com/articles/news_and_politics/politics/2012/05/americans_elect_an_inevitable_35_million_failure_.html.

232 Alex Wayne, "Obamacare Website Costs Exceed $2 Billion, Study Finds," *Bloomberg* (2014), http://www.bloomberg.com/news/articles/2014-09-24/obamacare-website-costs-exceed-2-billion-study-finds.

233 "Understanding the Effects of Internet Voting on Elections," *Internet Voting Project* (2014), http://www.internetvotingproject.com/.

234 Ibid.

235 Ibid.

236 Ibid.

237 Ibid.

238 Bob Bernick, "Utah Gop Set to File Suit against 'Count My Vote' Compromise," *utahpolicy.com* (2014), http://utahpolicy.com/index.php/features/today-

at-utah-policy/4104-utah-gop-set-to-file-suit-against-count-my-vote-compromise.

239 "Utah Gop Caucus Voters Praise Online Voting Experience," *Smartmatic* (2016), http://www.businesswire.com/news/financialpost/20160323006612/en/Utah-GOP-Caucus-Voters-Praise-Online-Voting.

240 Ibid.

241 Ibid.

242 Rich McCormick, "Utah's First Online Republican Primary Election Had Some Technical Problems," *The Verge* (2016), http://www.theverge.com/2016/3/23/11289484/utah-online-election-republican-primary-problems.

243 "Which One Is the Fake Internet Voting Site for Tonight's Utah Gop 'Online Caucus'?," *What Really Happened* (2016), http://whatreallyhappened.com/ru/content/which-one-fake-internet-voting-site-tonights-utah-gop-online-caucus#axzz43wdzSIX8.

244 Samira Saba, "Utah Gop Caucus Voters Praise Online Voting Experience," *Smartmatic* (2016), http://www.businesswire.com/news/financialpost/20160323006612/en/Utah-GOP-Caucus-Voters-Praise-Online-Voting.

245 Mark Thomas, telephone conversation with author, March 28, 2016.

246 Ibid.

247 Ibid.

248 Mike Summers, telephone conversation with author, March 29, 2016.

249 "Elections & Voting," *County of Los Angeles* (2016), https://www.lacounty.gov/government/elections-voting.

250 "Cities," *Los Angeles Almanac* (2016), http://www.laalmanac.com/cities/.

251 "Multilingual Services Program," *Los Angeles Country Register-Recorder/ County Clerk: Voting & Elections* (2016), http://www.lavote.net/home/ voting-elections/voter-education/multilingual-services-program/ multilingual-services-program.

252 Abby Sewell, "Touchscreen Ballots and a Choice in Polling Stations Could Be the Future of Voting in L.A. County," *Los Angeles Times* (2016), http://www.latimes. com/local/lanow/la-me-ln-county-voting-system-20160630-snap-story.html.

253 Ibid.

254 "Advisory Committees & Project Team," *Los Angeles Voting Systems Assessment Project* (2016), http://www.lavote.net/vsap/advisory-committees-project-team.

255 Michael Agresta, "Will the Next Election by Hacked?," *Wall Street Journal* (2012), http://www.wsj.com/articles/SB10000872396390444508504577595 280674870186.

256 "Los Angeles Selects Everyone Counts to Move Elections into the 21st Century with Secure Internet and Mobile Voting," *everyonecounts* (2015), http://www.everyonecounts.com/press-releases/los-angeles-selects-every-one-counts-to-move-elections-into-the-21st-century-with-secure-internet-and-mobile-voting.

257 "Empowerla," *City of Los Angeles Department of Neighborhood Empowerment* (2016), http://empowerla.org/onlinevoting/.

258 "The Travis County Clerk's Elections Division," *County of Travis. State of Texas* (2016), http://traviscountyclerk.org/eclerk/Content.do?code=Elections.

259 "Request for Information Star-Votetm a New Voting System," *TRAVIS COUNTY PURCHASING OFFICE* (2015), http://traviscountyclerk.org/eclerk/ content/images/pdf_STARVote_2015.06.03_RFI.pdf.

260 Elizabeth Weise, "Internet Voting Is Just Too Hackable, Say Security Experts," *USA Today* (2015), http://www.usatoday.com/story/tech/news/2016/01/28/internet-voting-not-ready-prime-time-security-risks/79456776/.

261 "Electronic Transmission of Ballots," *National Conference of State Legislatures* (2016), http://www.ncsl.org/research/elections-and-campaigns/internet-voting.aspx.

262 Ibid.

263 Lori Steele, telephone conversation with author, April 13, 2016.

264 Ibid.

265 "Online Election Perfection," *SimplyVoting* (2016), http://www.simply-voting.com.

266 "Easy, Secure, Anonymous Online Voting and Elections," *electionbuddy* (2016), http://electionbuddy.com/public/customers.

267 Lori Steele.

268 "Helios: Trust the Vote," *Helios Voting* (2016), https://vote.heliosvoting.org.

269 Ben Adida, email communication with author, June 28, 2016.

270 "About Smartmatic," *Smartmatic* (2016), https://www.smartmatic.com/about/.

271 Conny B. McCormack, "Democracy Rebooted: The Future of Technology in Elections: Video" (paper presented at the Atlantic Council, 2016).

272 "Remote Voting," *Scytl: Innovating Democracy* (2016), https://www.scytl.com/en/solutions/election-day/remote-voting/.

273 Satoshi Nakamoto, "Bitcoin: A Peer-to-Peer Electronic Cash System," (2008), https://bitcoin.org/bitcoin.pdf.

274 "State of Bitcoin and Blockchain 2016," *Coindesk* (2016), http://www.slide-share.net/CoinDesk/state-of-bitcoin-and-blockchain-2016-57577869.

275 Ibid.

276 Don Tapscott, "Blockchain and the Cio: A New Model for It," *LinkedIn* (2016), https://www.linkedin.com/pulse/blockchain-cio-new-model-don-tapscott?trk=hb_ntf_MEGAPHONE_ARTICLE_POST.

277 Peter Williams, "Blockchains in Government," ibid., https://www.linkedin.com/pulse/blockchains-government-peter-williams?trk=hp-feed-article-title-publish.

278 Melanie Swan, "Blockchain : Blueprint for a New Economy," (2015).

279 "Jerry Cuomo Says Blockchain Is Open for Business," *IBM Developer Works* (2016), https://developer.ibm.com/tv/videos/jerry-cuomo-says-blockchain-is-open-for-business/.

280 Ibid.

281 Telis Demos, "Bitcoin's Blockchain Technology Proves Itself in Wall Street Test," *Wall Street Journal* (2016), http://www.wsj.com/articles/bitcoins-blockchain-technology-proves-itself-in-wall-street-test-1460021421.

282 Selker, "Fixing the Vote: Electronic Voting Machines Promise to Make Fixing Elections More Accurate Than Ever before, but Only If Certain Problems—with the Machines and the Wider Electoral Process—Are Rectified".

283 Adam Ernest, email dialog with author, May 23, 2016.

284 Ibid.

285 "What Is a Benefit Corporation?," *Benefit Corporation* (2016), http://benefit-corp.net.

286 "Improved Technology and Better in-Person Interactions with Millennials Drive Historic Performance Improvement among Nation's Largest Retail Banks".

287 "Why Is Benefit Corp Right for Me?," *Benefit Corporation* (2016), http://benefitcorp.net/businesses/why-become-benefit-corp.

288 "E2e Verifiable Blockchain Voting Software -> Follow My Vote," *Kickstarter* (2016), https://www.kickstarter.com/projects/adamkalebernest/e2e-verifiable-blockchain-voting-software-follow-m/?&utm_source=website.

289 "Help Bring Honest Elections to the World," *Follow My Vote, Inc.* (2016), https://followmyvote.com.

290 Ibid.

291 Ibid.

292 Nick Spanos, telephone conversation with author, May 13, 2016.

293 Michael del Castillo, "Libertarian Party of Texas to Store Election Results on Three Blockchains," *Coindesk* (2016), http://www.coindesk.com/libertarian-party-texas-logs-votes-presidential-electors-blockchain/.

294 Nick Spanos.

295 Demos, "Bitcoin's Blockchain Technology Proves Itself in Wall Street Test".

296 "Statistics on Consumer Mobile Usage and Adoption to Inform Your Mobile Marketing Strategy Mobile Site Design and App Development," *Smart Insights* (2016), http://www.smartinsights.com/mobile-marketing/mobile-marketing-analytics/mobile-marketing-statistics/.

297 Linda M. Gallant, Gloria Boone, and Christopher S. LaRoche, "Mobile Usability: State of the Art and Implications," *nterdisciplinary Mobile Media and Communications* (2014).

298 "Mobile Retail E-Commerce Sales in the United States from 2013 to 2019 (in Billion U.S. Dollars)," *statista: The Statistics Portal* (2016), http://www. statista.com/statistics/249855/mobile-retail-commerce-revenue-in-the-united-states/.

299 Ben Adida.

300 Jason Soroko, "Playing in the Digital Sandbox: Mobile Versus Desktop Security," *Entrust* (2014), https://www.entrust.com/playing-digital-sandbox-mobile-versus-desktop-security/.

301 Surendra Thakur et al., "Experimentation Using Short-Term Spectral Features for Secure Mobile Internet Voting Authentication," *Mathematical Problems in Engineering* 2015 (2015).

302 Chris Savarese and Brian Hart, "The Caesar Cipher," *Cryptography* (2010), http://www.cs.trincoll.edu/~crypto/historical/caesar.html.

303 "The Fault, Dear Brutus, Is Not in Our Stars - Shakespeare Quotes," *e notes* (2016), http://www.enotes.com/shakespeare-quotes/fault-dear-brutus-our-stars.

304 Bruce Schneier, "NSA Surveillance: A Guide to Staying Secure," *theguardian* (2013), http://www.theguardian.com/world/2013/sep/05/nsa-how-to-remain-secure-surveillance.

305 Michael Cavna, "'Nobody Knows You're a Dog': As Iconic Internet Cartoon Turns 20, Creator Peter Steiner Knows the Idea Is as Relevant as Ever," *The Washington Post* (2013), https://www.washingtonpost.com/blogs/comic-riffs/post/nobody-knows-youre-a-dog-as-iconic-internet-cartoon-turns-20-creator-peter-steiner-knows-the-joke-rings-as-relevant-as-ever/2013/07/31/73372600-f98d-11e2-8e84-c56731a202fb_blog.html.

306 "About Touch Id Security on Iphone and Ipad," *Apple* (2016), https://support.apple.com/en-us/HT204587.

307 "Trojan Horse," *Encyclopedia Britannica* (2016), http://www.britannica.com/topic/Trojan-horse.

308 David Dill, telephone conversation with author, March 30, 2016.

309 Ibid.

310 Ibid.

311 "The Future of Voting: End-to_End Verifiable Internet Voting," *U.S. Vote Foundation* (2015), https://www.usvotefoundation.org/e2e-viv/summary.

312 Ibid.

313 Josh Benaloh, telephone and email conversations with author, June 3, 2016.

314 Selker, "Fixing the Vote: Electronic Voting Machines Promise to Make Fixing Elections More Accurate Than Ever before, but Only If Certain Problems—with the Machines and the Wider Electoral Process—Are Rectified".

315 "News & Updates," *Election Data Services* (2014), http://electiondataservices.com.

316 "Fixing the Vote: Electronic Voting Machines Promise to Make Fixing Elections More Accurate Than Ever before, but Only If Certain Problems—with the Machines and the Wider Electoral Process—Are Rectified".

317 "Online Voter Registration," *National Conference of State Legislatures* (2016), http://www.ncsl.org/research/elections-and-campaigns/electronic-or-online-voter-registration.aspx.

318 Ibid.

319 "We're No. 7!: US Drops Two Spots in E-Government Rankings," *Nextgov* (2014), http://www.nextgov.com/cio-briefing/2014/06/were-number-seven-us-ranks-top-ten-e-government-united-nations/87307/.

320 Janet Grenslitt, "Digital States Survey 2014 Results," *Center for Digital Government* (2014), http://www.govtech.com/cdg/digital-states/Digital-States-Survey-2014-Results.html.

321 John R. Patrick, *Health Attitude : Unraveling and Solving the Complexities of Healthcare* (Palm Coast, FL: Attitude LLC, 2015).

322 Fred Shapiro, "Follow the Money," *Freakonomics* (2011), http://freakonomics.com/2011/09/23/follow-the-money/.

323 David Goldman, "Apple's New $20 Billion Business," *CNN Money* (2016), http://money.cnn.com/2016/01/27/technology/apple-services/.

324 Benjamin Mayo, "Apple Music Now Has 13 Million Paying Subscribers, up from 11 Million in February," *9to5Mac* (2016), http://9to5mac.com/2016/04/26/apple-music-now-has-13-million-paying-subscribers-up-from-11-million-in-february/.

325 "Bitcoin Now Accepted by 100,000 Merchants Worldwide," *International Business Times* (2016), http://www.ibtimes.co.uk/bitcoin-now-accepted-by-100000-merchants-worldwide-1486613.

326 Jones and Simons, *Broken Ballots : Will Your Vote Count?*

327 "Hart Intercivic: Advancing Democracy," *Hart Intercivic* (2016), http://www.hartintercivic.com/content/about-hart.

328 Thomas G. Hansford and Brad T. Gomez, "Estimating the Electoral Effects of Voter Turnout," *The American Political Science Review* 104, no. 2 (2010).

329 Amber Phillips, "Why Hasn't Internet Voting Caught On? This Expert Has a Nefarious Theory.," *The Washington Post* (2016), https://www.washingtonpost.com/news/the-fix/wp/2016/03/24/why-havent-online-elections-caught-on-this-expert-has-a-nefarious-theory/?postshare=2061458823428350&tid=ss_mail.

330 Corbin Hiar, "Congressional Perks: Lawmakers' Most Surprising Benefits," *The Center for Public Integrity* (2016), https://www.publicintegrity.org/2011/11/23/7495/congressional-perks-lawmakers-most-surprising-benefits.

331 Joe Mohen, telephone conversation with author, March 28, 2016.

332 "Reelection Rates over the Years," *Center for Responsive Politics* (2015), https://www.opensecrets.org/bigpicture/reelect.php.

333 Andrew Dugan, "U.S. Congress and Its Leaders Suffer Public Discontent," *Gallup* (2015), http://www.gallup.com/poll/184556/congress-leaders-suffer-public-discontent.aspx?utm_source=Politics&utm_medium=newsfeed&utm_campaign=tiles.

334 "Congressional Job Approval," *RealClear Politics* (2016), http://www.realclearpolitics.com/epolls/other/congressional_job_approval-903.html.

335 Solveig Singleton, "How Cookie-Gate Crumbles," *Cato Institute* (2000), http://www.cato.org/publications/commentary/how-cookiegate-crumbles.

336 Donella H. Meadows and Rome Club de, *The Limits to Growth : A Report for the Club of Rome's Project on the Predicament of Mankind* (New York: Universe Books., 1972).

337 "Jay Wright Forrester," *Wikipedia* (2016), https://en.wikipedia.org/wiki/Jay_Wright_Forrester.

338 Elizabeth Weise, "Internet Voting Is Just Too Hackable, Say Security Experts," (2016), http://www.usatoday.com/story/tech/news/2016/01/28/internet-voting-not-ready-prime-time-security-risks/79456776/.

339 Barbara Simons and Douglas W. Jones, "Internet Voting in the U.S.," (2012), http://delivery.acm.org/10.1145/2350000/2347754/p68-simons.pdf?ip=75.69.126.253&id=2347754&acc=OPEN&key=4D4702B0C3E38B35%2E4D4702B0C3E38B35%2E4D4702B0C3E38B35%2E6D218144511F3437&CFID=612006

644&CFTOKEN=10726085&__acm__=1462635886_765a9845fbdd88a4e6e 9ed77233d7c69.

340 David Pogue, "Ssdp / Upnp," *Scientific American* (2016), http://www.scientifi- camerican.com/article/when-will-we-be-able-to-vote-online/.

341 Kirsten Anderson, "An Interview with David Wagner," *The Huffington Post* (2011), http://www.huffingtonpost.com/kirsten-anderson/an-interview-with-david-w_ b_64063.html.

342 "Verified Voting Board of Directors," *Verified Voting* (2014), https://www.veri- fiedvoting.org/board-of-directors/.

343 "Verified Voting Foundation: Principles for New Voting Systems," *Verified Voting* (2014), https://www.verifiedvoting.org/voting-system-principles/.

344 Pamela Smith, telephone conversation with author, June 1, 2016.

345 Ibid.

346 Ibid.

347 Patrick, *Net Attitude : What It Is, How to Get It, and Why You Need It More Than Ever*, 212-13.

348 "Utah Gop Caucus Voters Praise Online Voting Experience".

349 Conny B. McCormack, "Democracy Rebooted: The Future of Technology in Elections" (paper presented at the Atlantic Council, 2016).

350 Ibid.

351 Peter Haynes, "Online Voting: Rewards and Risks," *Atlantic Council: Brent Scowcroft Center on International Security* (2014), http://www.atlantic- council.org/images/publications/Online_Voting_Rewards_and_Risks. pdf.

352 Stephen Ansolabehere, email exchange with author, May 1, 2016.

353 Ibid.

354 Ibid.

355 Ibid.

356 Ibid.

357 McCormack, "Democracy Rebooted: The Future of Technology in Elections".

358 Conny Mccormack, email communication with author, July 10, 2016.

359 Ibid.

360 Michael Shamos, email communication with author, July 6, 2016.

361 Jeff Elder, "Latinos Lead U.S. Smartphone Use," *Wall Street Journal* (2014), http://blogs.wsj.com/digits/2014/02/10/latinos-lead-u-s-smartphone-use/.

362 Ibid.

363 Ibid.

364 Amy Chozick and Megan Thee-Brenan, "Poll Finds Voters in Both Parties Unhappy with Their Candidates," *New York Times* (2016), http://www.nytimes.com/2016/07/15/us/politics/hillary-clinton-donald-trump-poll.html?_r=0.

365 Michael Coblenz, "The Two-Party System Is Destroying America," *The Hill* (2016), http://thehill.com/blogs/congress-blog/politics/267222-the-two-party-system-is-destroying-america.

366 Sean Bryant, "How Much Will It Cost to Become President in 2016?," *Investope-dia* (2015), http://www.investopedia.com/articles/personal-finance/111815/how-much-will-it-cost-become-president-2016.asp.

367 Joseph Walker, "Drugmakers' Pricing Power Remains Strong," *Wall Street Journal* (2016), http://www.wsj.com/articles/drugmakers-pricing-power-remains-strong-1468488601.

368 Jerry Michalski, telephone conversation with author, June 6, 2016.

369 Ibid.

370 Ibid.

371 Cliff Zukin, "What's the Matter with Polling?," *New York Times* (2015), http://www.nytimes.com/2015/06/21/opinion/sunday/whats-the-matter-with-polling.html.

372 David Chaum, "Random Sample Voting," *rsvoting.org* (2009), http://rsvoting.org/whitepaper/white_paper.pdf.

373 Ibid.

374 Ibid.

375 Ibid.

376 Matt Canham, "Hatch Is under Fire for Helping Drugmaker," *The Salt Lake Tribune* (2013), http://www.sltrib.com/sltrib/politics/55686984-90/amgen-hatch-bill-legislation.html.csp.

377 "Switzerland's Voters Reject Basic Income Plan," *BBC News* (2016), http://www.bbc.com/news/world-europe-36454060.

378 Simon Kennedy, "Brexit Watch Indicators," *Bloomberg* (2016), http://www.bloomberg.com/graphics/2016-brexit-watch/.

379 Kelleher, *Internet Voting Now: Here's How, Here's Why, So You Can Kiss Citizens United Goodbye!*

380 Ibid.

381 "Ranked Choice Voting," *FairVote* (2014), http://www.fairvote.org/rankedchoicevoting#research_rcvamericanexperience.

382 Breana Noble, "Pros and Cons of Ranked-Choice Voting," *Newsmax* (2015), http://www.newsmax.com/FastFeatures/ranked-choice-voting-pros-and-cons/2015/07/03/id/653400/.

383 Rick Hasen, "2014 Eagleton Poll California Rcv Survey Results," *Election Law Blog* (2015), https://electionlawblog.org/?p=71773.

384 "Better Elections Are Possible," *FairVote For a More Perfect Union* (2016), http://www.fairvote.org.

385 "Ranked Choice Voting".

386 Vint Cerf, email communication with author, July 10, 2016.

387 Melissa Batchelor Warnke, "Silicon Valley, Forget the Apps and Fix Our Voting System," *Los Angeles Times* (2016), http://www.latimes.com/opinion/opinion-la/la-ol-silicon-valley-california-voting-election-primary-20160608-snap-20160608-snap-story.html.

388 Ibid.

389 Tennant, "Making the Case for Online Voting".

390 "U.S. Voter Turnout Trails Most Developed Countries".

391 Ibid.

Index